THE
MEANING
OF AUTHORITY

John E. Skinner

NIVERSITY
RESS OF
MERICA

Copyright © 1983 by

University Press of America, Inc.

P.O. Box 19101, Washington, D.C. 20036

ISBN (Perfect): 0-8191-3045-1
ISBN   (Cloth): 0-8191-3044-3

Copublished by arrangement with the
Episcopal Divinity School, Cambridge, Massachusetts

In Memory of My Father

ACKNOWLEDGEMENTS

Acknowledgement is made to the following for permission to quote from books which they have published: Charles Scribner's Sons for Martin Buber's I and Thou (R.G. Smith translation), 1955; Doubleday and Company for Avery Dulles' The Survival of Dogma, 1971; Random House for Loren Eiseley's The Immense Journey, 1961; The Macmillan Company for Alfred North Whitehead's Process and Reality, 1957; The United Reformed Church, London, England, for P.T. Forsyth's The Principle of Authority, 1952; The Alden Press for G.D. Yarnold's By What Authority?, 1964; The Seabury Press for James Cone's Black Theology and Black Power, 1969; Longman's, London England, for A.E.J. Rawlinson's Authority and Freedom, 1924; Harper and Row, Inc., for Sam Keen's Apology for Wonder, 1969; H.R. Niebuhr's Radical Monotheism and Western Culture, 1960; Mary Bosanquet's The Life and Death of Dietrich Bonhoeffer, 1968; and E.P. Dutton, Inc. for Blaise Pascal's Pensees (W.F. Trotter translation), 1941.   I should also like to thank the editor of The Review of Metaphysics for permission to quote from J.H. Randall, Jr.'s "Metaphysics and Language," (June 1967); the editor of Anglican Theological Review for permission to adapt and revise my article, "The Meaning of Authority," (January 1975); and the editor of The Witness for permission to adapt and revise my article, "Authority As Nurture," (July 1978).

TABLE OF CONTENTS

PREFACE

The problem of authority is a perennial one and no area of human inquiry is exempt from it. In this volume an attempt is made to deal with the meaning of authority within a Christian perspective, but an examination of philosophical and metaphysical structures, usually assumed in such discussions, is explicated as a key to understanding the meaning of authority. The inquiry is also placed within the context of a general analysis of culture and its various spheres of exertion.

My background in philosophical study initially was in the areas of German and American Idealism. In this respect Immanuel Kant and Josiah Royce were two important influences in the shaping of my thought. Through my teacher, Richard Kroner, these philosophical tenets were reinforced and also dethroned. In his critical philosophy of faith, based on the Judaeo-Christian revelation and tradition, all philosophical understanding was at the most penultimate in its possibilities for explanation. A posture of faith anchored in a revelatory focus was thus at least a potential liberation from philosophical and also theological pretensions.

Even such a posture, however, did not answer some important questions about the alienation between nature and human beings, and also the alienation of human beings from one another, and from the Divine Reality, or God. Here the works of Alfred North Whitehead have been particularly helpful in presenting possibilities for the healing of such isolation and alienation, and so process philosophy has come to be important for me in my work the past several years.

In this study on the meaning of authority, a critical philosophy of faith initially derived from Richard Kroner, certain emphases of liberation theology, and A.N. Whitehead's contribution, are in a sense combined. It is my contention that no contradiction is involved in this peculiar combination, although perhaps others may be able to discover loose ends of inconsistencies in the presentation.

No shortage of studies is present when dealing with the problem and meaning of authority. Vast resources are available and a select bibliography of some important titles is appended at the end of this book. Works by P.T. Forsyth, William W. Meissner, Yves R. Simon, and G.D. Yarnold have been particularly valuable resources for this study.

Finally, it has been my privilege to be able to test some of the ideas in this work with many of my colleagues at Episcopal Divinity School and the Boston Theological Institute, and I should like to thank, particularly, Hayden McCallum, Harold Oliver, and Edward Stiess for their sharing of criticism with me. In addition a number of other persons have made constructive suggestions about various aspects of this study.

They are: Fontaine Belford, John Knox, and Taylor Stevenson. I am grateful to them for their aid and support.

Episcopal Divinity School   JOHN E. SKINNER
Cambridge, Massachusetts

CHAPTER ONE

WHAT IS AUTHORITY?

Many human frustrations and dilemmas can be traced directly to a confusion centering around questions about authority. The word itself has had a bad reputation in that most forms of extrinsic authority are not trusted. Authority and its expressions in various societal structures are looked upon as oppressive, as threats to freedom, and as attempts to squelch genuine creativity and authentic feeling. Ivan Illich has demanded that in the future we must end the use of coercive power and authority,[1] and Illich is not the only person who equates authority with coercive power in our time.

In fact the facile equation of authority with coercion can lead to such questions as: Is authority distinct from coercive power or only a synonym for it? If authority has been seen as distinct from coercive power in the past, then, does such a reality currently exist? In other words, has authority disappeared from the present scene? Furthermore, if this is the case, has the vacuum caused by such a disappearance been filled by various kinds of organized coercion?

Answers to these questions do not come easily since many people do assume that authority and coercive power mean the same thing, and thus there is no problem to be considered. Hannah Arendt, the distinguished political philosopher, is one of those who does make a distinction between authority and coercive power. In an important discussion of this issue she states that because authority always demands obedience, it is commonly mistaken for some form of power or violence, but it is her contention that the nature of authority precludes the use of external means of coercion.[2] In fact, if such coercion is used, authority itself has failed or has ceased to be.[3] At the same time Arendt is convinced that authority has disappeared in our time because of the loss of primordial sources for it. Such sources provide for a common experience and are anchored in an arche (beginning) derived from a constellation of events which provides a direction for the future and a need for recollection on the past. In most instances also these events serve as a way of focusing ultimate reality.

In theological language, such events are called revelation. In the modern secular world, however, such revelatory or quasi-revelatory events are not viable, so the powermongers in some instances have their day, and those who do prevail attempt to invent modern myths to take the place of revelation and as a result reinforce their power. This can also be expressed by saying that authority ultimately is based on faith, and when the images and models of ultimate reality are lost, then, all sorts of substitutes come in and take their place. Whether or not Hannah Arendt is correct in her judgment concerning the disappearance of authority, her conclusions are important as attempts to come to grips with these issues continue.

Another way of investigating these questions centers in a consideration of two models for human community. The first model is the organic one based on a familial context. Here the child is born into an already existent community and this familial community is necessary for the child's nurture and care. A long period of maturation necessitates the child's dependence on such a community, and the emergence into personhood by the child means that this community must be concerned with the child's growth and eventual adulthood. The child as dependent is obedient to the family unit (mother, father, etc.). In the beginning of the child's experience all of reality is probably equated with this unit and it is only through gradual growth that the limits to such a reality are discovered.

When these limits are revealed, then, tensions may develop between the familial matrix and the reality outside this unit. This also is necessary for the eventual emergence into personhood. Consequently, when the child is able to affirm its past dependence, and also assert a present relative independence, it is on the way towards self-dependence and genuine freedom. All sorts of difficulties may arise in this process. The familial matrix may become a post-natal womb protecting the child from the reality outside unduly, and as a result the child/adult may have to take violent measures to make its break from such a smothering atmosphere into individuality and personhood.

The second model is a mechanistic one based on theories of social contract. Here the individual or person who has emerged from the familial or organic type of community contracts for involvement in a number of possible groups. By the very nature of this sort of contractural arrangement the person may keep his distinctness as an individual to a certain extent, but the person must surrender some of his relative freedom or individual sovereignty to the universality of the group itself. If the particular group has built within it structures designed to minimize this surrender, then, the loss of freedom will also be slight; but if not, then the worst aspects of this kind of involvement may result in a depersonalized, distinct unit (the former individual) making its contribution to the whole. Furthermore, the so-called social self, _esprit de_ _corps_, becomes the true individual, even in a sense the true person, and what was before a relatively free individual person has now become transformed into merely a part or an expression of the group's social self.

The mechanistic aspect of this model should be obvious since machines which function well must have distinct parts which make individual contributions to the whole, but do not find themselves distinguished from the whole. In the first organic model the potential individual or person is nurtured in a social, familial matrix whose purpose is to allow the emergence of free personhood, but this is often obstructed by a smothering rather than a nurturing effect from the organic matrix. In contrast to the organic model the mechanistic one changes relatively free personhood into a distinct, abstract unit which must fit into the totality of the social machine itself. Aberrant behavior in the first instance is viewed as a threat to the health of the organic matrix, and in the second instance, it is seen as destructive to the smooth functioning of the mechanistic entity, however it may be constructed.

It is undoubtedly true that both of these models for human community appear to be inadequate. A community in which personhood is shaped and nurtured; the breakthrough into relative freedom is fostered; coupled with an interpersonal or intersubjective dynamic between relatively free persons; resulting in a mutual interdependence which does not occasion pathological dependence but healthy freedom; is what should be the case. Whether or not such human community is a political or moral possibility is one of the crucial issues for any period of history. Such a model of human community has been in the past promulgated primarily by eschatological visions of people of faith and not by political planners or even by utopian visionaries whose models for community almost always in the end involve the primacy of the group or the group's social self over the relatively free person or individual.

For our purposes we shall recognize the relative importance and value of both the organic and mechanistic models of community, and use the third possibility which is derived primarily from the Judaeo-Christian tradition as a criterion of judgment in the recognition of the limits of the other two models. The third possibility as described is not wholly characteristic of any empirical, historical communities- secular or religious, even though some claims have been made to the contrary. The so-called classic or Catholic model of ecclesiastical community characteristic of Roman, Orthodox, Anglican, Lutheran, and some other Protestant bodies, is primarily organic in its makeup, while sectarian models of ecclesiastical community (groups having their origin in the Radical Reformation of the sixteenth century as well as some others) tend to resemble the other alternative. In neither case has the vision of the reign of God been completely realized.

It is certainly in connection with an examination of models for human community that the questions concerning the meaning of authority are pertinent. What is authority? Or what was authority?

In the Christian Faith authority is anchored fully in the reality of God. All questions of authority which we ask ultimately have their referent in the Divine Reality. Both Jews and Christians have been taught a great deal about the reality of God. We both affirm that the source of our being is identical with the source of our meaning. Another way to express this is simply that the One who creates us also redeems and liberates us, the One who gives us our life may also make that life worth living. Worth is an intrinsic aspect of existence and being. God is the creator and preserver of all humankind.

Both Jewish and Christian believers should be able to affirm the present reality of authority because of the constellation of events centering in Moses and the prophets and in Jesus of Nazareth, and the revelation disclosed there which expresses that through the divine creative activity there is implicit a nurturing and liberating presence. God expresses his presence in the totality of the creation, both in nature and in history. In Christian Faith and theology, this dynamic divine activity has been called the Word of God. And this Word of God, this nurturing and liberating presence, is definitely revealed for Christians in the constellation of events centered in Jesus Christ.

A criterion for authority can be found for the Christian in these affirmations of faith.[4] All authority is derived from God, derived from his nurturing and liberating presence in nature and in history. Consequently, all authority should express itself as both a nurturing and liberating presence reflecting its ultimate source in the creative and redemptive activity of God. The Gospel of Christ, as a result, becomes the criterion for the Christian in order to determine whether authority is present, or only organized power parading as authority.

Many social structures, both secular and religious, express this nurturing and liberating function and serve as ways for bringing worth and meaning to human life. An Anglican theologian uttered many years ago a commonplace statement that perhaps needs to be declared again: "It is obvious that in every sphere of human interest and in every relationship of human life, the individual is largely moulded by the social tradition which he inherits, and by the spiritual environment into which he is born; and that Authority is the inevitable form under which education and social training begin."[5] A more recent thinker affirms such a view when he states: "It would appear that the mature man, whether religious or non-religious, chooses to credit the context that nourishes and creates him as being worthy of trust, and this is the source of the ability to relax and act gracefully. The alternative to such an act of faith is resentment, which leads to the view that the world is alien and hostile to the human spirit."[6]

From the above discussion a context of nurture leading to redemption or liberation (making free) is posited as the necessary condition for human maturation. If the context in question does not nurture, and thus does not evoke gratitude on the part of the one being nurtured, then something is distinctively wrong with the agency and thus with the authority in question. If trust is not an emergent from the context of authority, if resentment arises, then this means that nurture has probably ceased, liberation is not possible, and oppression has begun. So, presumably, authority should occasion trust and gratitude, not rebellion

4

and resentment. If the latter occurs, then, the authority is in jeopardy, since it has failed in its fundamental task.

The question, however, of what constitutes oppression and enslavement is a difficult one. Certainly, rigid structures have existed and do exist which demand conformity to them at the expense of the individual's integrity and the sacrifice of his selfhood. But this does not mean that all objections to structures as being oppressive are equally valid. The flesh is often weak when it is subjected to a disciplining influence; it may speak of being oppressed when in reality it is not; and yet, without cultivation, without discipline, without nurture, liberation resulting in freedom, selfhood and personhood is impossible.

This may be illustrated by a brief discussion of the relation of spontaneity and freedom. It is often said today that to be free is to be spontaneous, to assert yourself without restraint, to feel deeply without mediating influences, to be immediate and thus honest and authentic. Spontaneity is thus affirmed to be one of the blessed virtues of our present time. A careful analysis of the meaning of the word, spontaneity, uncovers almost a direct opposite of what is intended. Take a given person. He is spontaneous in his response to something. On the surface he appears to be free and unrestricted. Below the surface, however, he is only acting compulsively, which is of course the opposite of freedom. In fact one of the Greek words for spontaneity so understood is to automaton. Yves Simon asserts that in spontaneity things take care of themselves, and this expression which belongs to the language of daily life conveys with precision the Aristotelian idea of a situation in which the desirable result is brought about spontaneously, automatically, without anyone having had to intend it, or to arrange things according to intention.[7]

It may be possible that in current word usage spontaneity can be understood as a self-controlled intensity, which is the opposite of automatic behaviour, but with this exception one might conclude that spontaneous action is action without a centered self, action which automatically acts out what is already implicit in the past of the organism (or individual) in question. If this is true, then, social structures which attempt to shape and nurture the organism (or individual) in the direction of a centered selfhood are necessary in order for freedom to result. Freedom, thus, cannot be identified with automatic, unrestrained behavior, no matter how exciting, or how wonderful it may appear at the moment to the sentient organism. Spontaneity, understood in this way, is nothing more than "conformal feeling," to use an expression of Alfred North Whitehead's.

If such a conclusion is correct, then, freedom arises through cultivation by societal structures and becomes that reality which breaks through these structures, setting up a healthy tension between authority and freedom. Thus "real authority requires real freedom as the only environment in which it can live."[8] Or to put it another way, Auguste Sabatier writes:

> Historic authority demands at once respect and criticism; respect because, being the expression of a given tradition, custom, social state, it brings us an inheritance by which we have profited and shall continue to profit: criticism, because by elevating our conscience and reason, this very authority no longer represents anything other than a bygone phase of evolution. Authority in its true conception, is, and can be no other than relative.[9]

Based on the preceding discussion, the following tentative definition of authority is posited: That kind of structured reality, whether societal or personal, which through nurture and cultivation enables individuals to become truly centered selves or persons, and thus, relatively free beings. This definitation is not in conflict with and is supported by one developed by G.D. Yarnold: "The best we can do is to define 'authority' as that intrinsic quality which by right claims the respect and reverence of mankind generally."[10]

Such a definition of authority is anchored in the Gospel criterion, and such a criterion can be used for valuing the presence of such authority in the multiple cultural activities of human beings such as scientific inquiry, artistic creation, political planning, moral struggle, and religious commitment. Furthermore, such a criterion may be used for judging the pretensions of scientism, aestheticism, statism, moralism, and ecclesiasticism.

Since authority for the Christian is anchored in faith and the Gospel criterion, let me now select one symbol for authority from among the many appropriate symbols which come from the Christian Faith and which embody the Gospel criterion. Let us test it out on the basis of what has been concluded about authority and the projected definition of authority.

The symbol is shepherd. In our tradition God has been imaged as a shepherd, Jesus Christ is the Good Shepherd, and Christians in some traditions look to their bishops and pastors as shepherds, and they often see such a symbol as the shepherd's crook, the bishop's crozier.

In the Biblical tradition the shepherd is one who cares for all his sheep, who seeks them out if they are lost, who knows them by name, and who provides them with protection and nurture, and who at times risks his life on their behalf. In the Book of Ezekiel (34: 11-17 NEB) God is identified as a shepherd. "Now I myself will ask after my sheep and go in search of them. I will search for the lost, recover the straggler, bandage the hurt, strengthen the sick, and leave the healthy and strong to play.[11]

6

This is, theologically, a remarkable identification, if we would only take it seriously -- the God who searches out the lost, the God who recovers the straggler, the God who permits the healthy and the strong to play. The difficulty is that Christians often do not believe this. As Whitehead has observed, the tender vision of Galilean humility was replaced in Christian tradition by the overpowering imagery of Caesar's court. The attributes of Caesar became the attributes of God and also of the shepherd, and Christians have been trying to adapt the Biblical wisdom of God concerning his nurturing and liberating presence to these attributes of Caesar for hundreds of years. God is immutable, God is impassible, God is omnipotent, we were often taught in the past. And yet if we confronted another human being who acted as though he were immutable, we would classify that person as rigid; or if we met one who is impassible, we would find a person without warmth, without feeling. A human monster, no less! Even so, such attributes have been applied to God. Fortunately, the Bible knows better and the Gospel criterion can free us from such affirmations, even though such imagery has influenced our views of secular and religious authority.

This imagery of God as shepherd is focused poignantly in the New Testament. Jesus Christ, God's Son, is the Good Shepherd who gives his life for the sheep. In Jesus the imagery of the caring God, the loving God, the God who searches and finds, is definitely expressed. In the New Testament the image of such a Christ opens up the reality of God for us, and those of us who would be Christian disciples, find that God claims us in this manner, not as the overpowering ruler, but as the tender shepherd, not as the remote monarch, but as one who is with us (Emmanuel). This is dramatized in the exchange between Jesus and Peter in John 21. Peter, who had denied Jesus three times before his crucifixion, is searched out and confronted with the Divine Love, and Peter affirms that love three times, and he is then directed to feed the sheep, to nurture and care for them, to be one of the shepherds of Christ. In I Peter (5: 1-4 NEB) we hear an admonition directed to the shepherds of Christ: "Tend that flock of God whose shepherds you are, and do it, not under compulsion, but of your own free will, as God would have it, not for gain, but out of sheer devotion; not tyrannizing over those who are allotted to your care, but setting an example to the flock."

Consequently, the God who searches out his people, who wrestles with the forces of evil on their behalf, the God who is revealed as the Man on the Cross, continues to express his love and care through all those societal structures which convey a nurturing and liberating presence, and through those persons who as shepherds and servants of God search out the people, and express through their lives the ultimate acceptance of the God they serve.

The crucial questions are these: Are Christians going to let the Gospel be the criterion for forming images of God or not? Are Christians going to permit the Gospel to be the criterion for views of both secular and ecclesiastical authority or not? The answers to these questions are very difficult to achieve. A part of the Christian moral struggle is precisely involved in an attempt to answer in the affirmative. An answer in the negative would have devastating consequences as past history has demonstrated.

The late British theologian, P.T. Forsyth, once said that if reality be not redemptive, it is not moral,[12] and it follows that if reality is not redemptive, then it is alien to the human moral struggle for personhood. Such an alien reality, however it may be understood or whatever structure it may have due to human cultural exertion, must be resisted by human beings committed to the moral struggle.

Many societal structures, both secular and religious, often appear to be alien to the human moral struggle. They have the character of imposing organizations or power solely interested in the maintenance of that power. They are apparently oblivious to the struggle of the outcast, of the neglected, of those without recognition and without worth (non-persons) in the eyes of all of those protected within the powerful structures. These societal structures represent reality for large numbers of people, but they are alien because they do not mediate a nurturing and liberating presence. They are rather a smothering and oppressive force holding human beings back from full personhood thus prematurely stopping the moral struggle. The power structure becomes the substitute for God's nurturing and liberating presence.

When such an alien blockage of reality finally begins to crumble, the people within it are bewildered and frustrated, faced with the disintegration of the only reality they ever knew. When this happens, it is a crucial time for genuine authority to act, for genuine authority to nurture, cultivate, and enable the affirmation of a deeper faith in the Divine Reality which transcends organizations of power, and affirms the only genuine authority, the authority of the Divine creative and redemptive activity.

In conclusion, when Christians through their faith can affirm such authority, then this authority expresses itself (a) as a prophetic witness against those organized powers which smother and oppress, and (b) as a witness for and an actual involvement in the nurturing and liberating presence which enables individuals to become centered persons with relative freedom. Moreover, the community of Christians, the Church, expresses its authority as a priestly medium only when it conveys the nurturing and liberating presence of the Divine Reality. This Reality is the ultimate source for all human authority, and the ultimate judge against all sinful distortions of authority.

8

NOTES: Chapter One.

1.   Ivan D. Illich, Celebration of Awareness (New York: Doubleday and Company, 1970), p. 17.

2.   Hannah Arendt, Between Past and Future (New York: Penguin Books, 1968), pp. 91-141.

3.   Ibid., pp. 92-93.

4.   Since it is my contention that authority is ultimately rooted in faith and in the 'object' of faith, criteria for authority may be found in traditions of faith other than the Christian one.   As far as authority is concerned, an identity of creator and redeemer (liberator), or being and worth, or fact and value, would seem to be necessary in these traditions if the thesis of this discussion is a sound one.

5.   A.E.J. Rawlinson, Authority and Freedom (London: Longmans, Green and Company, 1924), p. 3.   Used by permission of the publisher.

6.   Sam Keen, Apology for Wonder (New York: Harper and row, 1969), p. 206. Used by permission of the publisher.

7.   Yves R. Simon, A General Theory of Authority (Notre Dame, Indiana: University of Notre Dame Press, 1962), p. 116.

8.   Rawlinson, Authority and Freedom, p. 17.   Used by permission.

9.   Auguste Sabatier, Religions of Authority and the Religion of the Spirit, trans. L.S. Houghton (New York: McClure, Phillips and Company, 1904), pp. xvii-xviii.

10.   G.D. Yarnold, By What Authority? (London: A.R. Mowbray and Company, 1964), p. 4.   Within this book Yarnold presents a brief etymological analysis of authority.   He finds that the word "authority" comes from the root verb in Latin augere which means first of all to increase, enlarge, and augment, thus magnifying and exalting that which is already in existence.   And, consequently, the one who increases his possessions and his power is deemed worthy of high honor.   Thus augere takes on the meaning of to reverence, or to worship by offerings of tribute.   Correspondingly, auctor signifies one who brings about the existence of an object or promotes its prosperity and is thus deemed to possess auctoritas, a dignity or reputaton or eminence which secures the right to the reverence and tribute of human beings. By What Authority?, p. 1. Used by permission of the publisher.

11.   All Scriptural passages are taken from the New English Bible.

12.   P.T. Forsyth, The Principle of Authority (London: Independent Press, Ltd., 1952), p. 129. Used by permission of the publisher.

CHAPTER TWO

AUTHORITY, GOD, AND HUMAN BEINGS

Several years ago a school teacher in Iowa achieved a degree of notoriety by proving how conditioning affects the performance level of third graders. In an effort to teach children from a homogeneous culture what it means to suffer discrimination she announced one day that she had discovered that her brown-eyed pupils were much less bright than their blue-eyed counterparts. These unfortunates were then made to wear an identifying collar, and for the next week were singled out for every sort of humiliation. Significantly, in that brief period, the children began to show the effects of treatment. Their grades fell, they became alternately belligerent and depressed, they were unable to concentrate either in the classroom or the playground. When the roles were reversed and the blue-eyed children were turned against, precisely the same thing happened.

The image of ourselves which we make a part of our inwardness in the course of our growing up controls profoundly our capacities to do and be. In large part our external behavior is simply a manisfestation of the self we have been taught to feel we are. This self has to do with private experiences; "My brother William excels in academic subjects. Everyone says so."; family experience, "We Edwards are always good at mathematics"; group experience, "Frances Willard is the worst school in the system, and has the weakest students."; religious experience, "The day of the Lord is a day of doom!" Because of the solemnity of the context in which it is presented, the cultural weight which it is given to bear, and the naturally intense and profound nature of the experiences with which it resonates, the image of God which Christian believers acknowledge probably has more to do than anything else with how they understand themselves and their lives. It is extraordinary how many religiously "indifferent" intellectuals seem to be haunted by the God shaped within them so long ago. They may not be able to forgive such a being, but no more can that Divine Image be forgotten.

When we talk about authority in Christian perspective, we must seek to understand how people interpret themselves in relation to themselves, to one another, to nature, and to God. We cannot achieve a selfhood, which manifests a sense of the interconnectedness of all life, a healthy wholeness and freedom, when the God in whom we believe and who is the source of all authority is oppressive, or abstract; angry, or indifferent; damning, or absent. We cannot achieve a state of healthy freedom when God takes more from us than is given to us, or gives more than we can take; when the Divine Reality is without motion, or without rest.

One of the fundamental difficulties which we face in coming to grips with a Christian understanding of authority is how to develop a view of God or ultimate reality which does justice to our concern for a healthy freedom and the affirmation of the nurturing and liberating presence, and yet does not fall prey to traditional theological distortions. These distortions have been many in the history of theological and philosophical inquiry, and perhaps can be summarized by a dictum made famous by Alfred North Whitehead in Process and Reality.[1] It is Whitehead's conviction that the proper solution to the theological and philosophical quest can only come through an adequate synthesis of ultimacy and immediacy, of universality and individuality. Most systematic attempts have lost one pole in the other, or have subordinated in an unwarranted fashion the individual or particular to the universal, or vivid immediacy to abstract ultimacy. Furthermore, as we have seen, this philosophical and theological concern is evident in our attempt to deal with authority and freedom.

Whitehead finds this conflict to be most evident when examining various models of Deity. In the New Testament we are confronted with a Galilean vision of humility expressed in the figure of Jesus of Nazareth. It dwells "on the tender elements in the world which slowly and in quietness operate by love, and it finds purpose in the present immediacy of a kingdom not of this world. Love neither rules, nor is it unmoved; also it is a little oblivious as to morals."[2] As we have seen for Christians the definitive revelation of God is expressed in the life and death of Jesus of Nazareth and this haunting vision has continued to persist throughout the centuries despite many obstacles.

These obstacles are seen in the vain attempt of some traditional theologies to synthesize such a vision of ultimate reality (God) with other models of Deity which are in direct contradiction to the tender and delicate revelation in Jesus. Whitehead delineates three such models as being prominent in this incredible alliance. First, God is portrayed as an imperial ruler based on the image of Caesar. When such a model is used, the revelation in Jesus tends to be characterized by a weighty omnipotence, and cloaked in an extrapolated imagery of the Imperial Court. Another model is that of God as a ruthless moralist. This comes from an exaggeration and distortion of certain emphases in the Old Testament, particularly that of immutability. Finally, God becomes the personification of a philosophical principle, the Absolute or unmoved mover of Book XII of Aristotle's Metaphysics. God here is the ultimate abstraction , totally unaware of anything other than itself. Aristotle's God is the thought which thinks itself in splendid isolation. Since to know what is not perfect is to be imperfect, this God is not aware that it moves those lesser realities -- attracted erotically to its divine perfection. Thus it is utterly impassible. The God with which these images leave us is thus omnipotent, immutable, immovable -- a far cry from the incarnate Christ, the suffering servant of Isaiah, weeping over Jerusalem.

Voices such as those of Whitehead, Charles Hartshorne, and Norman Pittenger among others have called attention to these contradictions but it has been difficult to hear them over the heavy shouting of neo-orthodox and fundamentalist theologians. But when the shouting has died down, perhaps we shall be in a better position to listen.

In the recent past we have seen, among other anomalies, the rise of the so-called death-of-God theology. This perspective is too involved to describe in detail here,[3] but it certainly is true that one of its principal emphases is the negation of models of deity such as we have just described. One representative even equates such an image of God with Satan.[4]

Current feminist thought on this subject, such as found in Mary Daly's Beyond God the Father, also manifests a violent distaste for a model of deity which is defined by an omnipotent, immutable, impassible, male image of the Imperial Caesar. The erroneous equation of the term "Loving Father" with such a model destroys the potential which the image of a loving father might have in mediating the nurturing and liberating presence of ultimacy. Instead, it transforms the word "father" into a synonym for arrogance, coldness, domination, aloofness, coercive power, and negates the tenderness, warmth, gentleness, affection and love which might be seen as feminine aspects of ultimacy.[5]

The development of a view of God or ultimate reality which does justice to our concern for a healthy freedom is a crucial factor in our coming to terms with a Christian understanding of authority. It may be that the best we can do is to clear away a lot of conceptual brush which now hampers our task, and then to posit a few suggestions for future consideration which, if coupled with an attitude of reverence and prayer, may result in the gift of a new insight, image, or model of God or ultimate reality. Perhaps we may be able to recover what has been implicit in the revelation of God in Jesus of Nazareth all along, but lost through human sinfulness and pretension -- a God characterized by a "tenderness which loses nothing that can be saved, and a wisdom which uses what in the temporal world has been mere wreckage."[6]

Consequently, the influence of models of God upon views which have been developed about nature and human beings is without question an important consideration. The Aristotelian thought which thinks itself in splendid isolation has been transformed into the cold, calculating, technical reason of modern humanity which strips reality of all dimensions which are not subject to quantification, and leaves us with a nature and a world, devoid of feeling, of rhythm, of pulsation. This "new creation," which is very much the reflection of its inventors, bears little resemblance to that world of nature which was a sacramental medium for the presence of ultimacy, in which even the most elemental forms of life constituted a mystery if allowed to be themselves, rather than transformed into abstract units of a mechanistic scheme.

The modern technical thinker may become like his image of God an unmoved mover, an impassible analyst, an immutable observer of a facticity devoid of value. All dimensions of reality which cannot be contained within the confines of this vision are sloughed off as nonsensical, as emotive, as irrational.

The source of this incredible deformation is most obviously found in the contribution which Rene Descartes has made to our modern world. His famous dualism between thought (res cogitans) and extension (res extensa) gives the kind of philosophical and scientific structuring needed for transforming nature from a vibrant organic reality into a vast inert mechanism.

The res cogitans, the thinking thing, which is an abstraction from the wholeness of human being, is primarily a human thought which thinks itself in splendid isolation. Descartes came up with this discovery while shut up in a stove.

The res extensa, the extended thing, is the reduced nature which results from the application of mathematical categories to the vast and overwhelming reality of nature. This nature (a creation of the human thought which thinks itself) is devoid of feeling, is devoid of any conceptual or mental aspect, is devoid of any value; it is the fixed, measurable, quantifiable mechanism which ruled until recently in scientific inquiry.[7] A startling example of the brutal aspects of such a creation is seen in the subordination of all sentient creatures, except of course the human thought which thinks itself, to the status of clogs in nature's vast engine. As a result of this debasement the attitude developed that animals had no feeling, thus suffered no pain, and therefore could be subjected to the most demonic of tortures. When they cried out in agony, they were not really feeling anything. Machines do not feel; they function!

The effect of such philosophic brutality cannot be minimized. The dissociation of sensibility,[8] which caused a split in the human reality, could go from an insensitivity to the feeling implicit in the so-called inert stuff of nature, to an insensitivity to plant feeling and animal feeling, and finally, to an insensitivity to human feeling, particularly any human feeling not acceptable on the basis of some predetermined cultural, social, racial, or sexual bias.

The model of God as a ruthless moralist derived from an exaggeration and distortion of the prophetic emphasis in the Old Testament has plagued the modern world by its many incarnations in a number of moralistic tyrants who have sought to destroy the vivid immediacy of living under the gun of moral abstractions.[9] The important tension between moral laws (universality) and particular contexts (individuality) has been lost through a negation of the latter. The result has been a personal rigidity which has done immeasurable damage to the psychological health of countless people, and which has resulted in an equally distressing reaction: the loss of moral law (universality) and the adoption of aesthetic immediacy as a substitute for moral integrity and uprightness.

The model of God expressed as an imperial ruler based on the image of Caesar has been a source of distress throughout history in its many incarnations. Particularly in the twentieth century, we have seen such a model become flesh in figures where the coercive power of a despot is wedded to a transcendence of moral direction, and thus finding himself beyond good and evil becomes a trans-moral conscience gone mad.[10] Two particular expressions of this kind of monstrosity are of course Adolf Hitler and Josef Stalin. How many more are lurking in the shadows, surfacing at times; madmen who with a lust for power will play the destroyer, and pull all reality into themselves; the imperial God dwelling with us as the despotic enemy -- God, literally, becoming Satan with us.

Consequently, the way we view God has an overwhelming effect on our views of community, on the methods we use for shaping and teaching human beings, on our attitudes towards nature, and our attitudes towards one another. The equation of absolute despotic power with the Divine Reality will influence our concepts of authority, and often has resulted in the equation of authority with coercive power. It is therefore fitting that we develop a brief philosophic overview of such an equation and its effects on nature and human beings since the seventeenth century. Through this examination of the past, it is hoped that fresh insights concerning nature, human beings, and God will enable us to gain a sounder approach to the meaning of authority, and will make it possible for us as Christians to affirm the ultimate source of authority as the nurturing and liberating presence of the Divine Reality.

We have seen that the Cartesian abstraction from human being (res cogitans) and the reduction of nature to quantifiable extension (res extensa) has resulted in a dualistic perspective which it is almost impossible to correct as long as we work within its framework. In DesCartes' scheme the human body is subsumed under the category of mechanized nature, while the human mind (or soul?) is the thinking thing. Both body and mind are abstractions from human wholeness.

In the seventeenth century a contemporary of Descartes, Blaise Pascal, himself a distinguished mathematician and paradoxically the actual inventor of the first thinking thing, a calculating machine, developed a violent distaste for the abstractions of Cartesian philosophy. When confronted by its monstrous distortion of nature and of human beings, Pascal declared with an emotional fervor which itself became a living refutation of such aberrations, "The heart has its reasons which reason does not know. We feel it in a thousand things.."[11] This expression, and many others like it, witnessed to that vast reservoir of possibility which had been excluded in the reductionism of the Cartesians. The heart became the symbol for that vast reservoir, and reason served as the image for the technical reduction of reality to thought and extension. Here the bifurcation between conceptuality and feeling became apparent, and it was Pascal's intention to affirm the possibiltiy of feeling, "we feel it in a thousand things."

Pascal, furthermore, did not see a dualism between body and mind as an accurate explanation of human nature. Rather a duality developed (not a dualism) between the human possibility for grandeur and the human possibility for misery. The human person hovers between angel and brute, and "he who would act the angel acts the brute."[12] He also anticipated a dynamic view of human nature, first in his affirmation of the heart and human feeling, and secondly in his remarkable statement, "Our nature consists in motion; complete rest is death."[13]

Pascal affirmed a human wholeness achieved through the creative and redemptive action of the living God revealed in Jesus of Nazareth. The grandeur and misery of humankind is expressed vividly in the life and death of the Galilean, and this life and this death becomes a model for the reality of God.

It was Pascal's contention that philosophers have consecrated the vices by placing them in God,[14] whereas Christian believers should consecrate the virtues in a vision of the Divine Being focused in Jesus of Nazareth. To equate God with the Imperial Caesar, or to describe God as a ruthless moralist, is to identify God with vices born of human power. Pascal's insistence on the rejection of the God of the philosophers is due, furthermore, to the recognition that such a god is a pale abstraction, even a distortion of the Divine Reality. When reason is reduced and limited to abstract, quantifiable calculation, then "it is the heart which experiences God, and not the reason. This, then, is faith; God felt by the heart, not by the reason."[15]

The revelation of God in Jesus of Nazareth, that Galilean vision of humility, that discovery in the Divine Reality of a tenderness which loses nothing that can be saved, and a wisdom which uses what in the temporal world has been mere wreckage, that revelation stands in judgment upon such a reconstruction of nature and human beings, and implicitly on past distorted images of the Divine Reality.[16] In the mind and heart of Pascal such distortions were vetoed with a vehemence which still rings in the ears of sensitive people. Pascal, until recently, was dismissed as a philosopher; few histories of philosophy gave him much if any attention; but his veto of philosophic brutality and pretension still stands, and his witness to the revelation of God in Jesus of Nazareth is pertinent today: "The God of Abraham, the God of Isaac, the God of Jacob, the God of Christians, is a God of love and comfort, a God who fills the soul and heart of those whom he possesses, a God who makes them conscious of their inward wretchedness, and his infinite mercy, who unites himself to their inmost soul, who fills it with humility and joy, with confidence and love, who renders them incapable of any other end than himself."[17]

In the eighteenth century Immanuel Kant was faced with a number of dilemmas which his critical philosophy was designed to dispel. He was the inheritor of a philosophic tradition derived from Descartes, Spinoza and Leibniz on the Continent, and in great Britain, Locke, Berkeley and Hume. He was also confronted by a reduced picture of nature as mechanism which was characteristic of the reigning Newtonian physics.

Newton's mechanistic view of nature, comparable to Descartes' res extensa, was the product of a reduced understanding of human reasoning which reflected the Cartesian res cogitans. In the Kantian philosophy the attempt was first made to determine how knowledge of such a mechanistic nature was possible. This was the task of The Critique of Pure Reason. In this Critique the conditions which made possible a knowledge of the objects in the mechanistic scheme were also seen as the conditions which made possible the objects themsleves. Kant was clear in his discovery that the mechanistic view of nature was in one sense at least a fabrication of the human technical reason. When reason is reduced to its theoretical function, then the only reality possible is the measurable mechanism, devoid of value and feeling, which was the then regnant Weltbild. Such a picture of the world was an abstraction from wholeness and the reflection of a reduced selfhood which produced the model.

At the same time Kant was very much aware that Pascal's vast reservoir of human possibility symbolized by the heart was neglected in such a theoretical construct of nature. Since such a construct of nature was dominant at that time, in order to explain or to include the neglected dimensions Kant substituted for Pascal's "heart" his concept of the practical reason. What was not accessible to the analytic function of the theoretical reason was indeed presupposed in human inquiry, and concepts of wholeness, such as self, world, and God, were in Kant's language at least regulative ideas of the practical sphere, making possible theoretical knowledge.[18]

A duality in Kant's thought arises between the theoretical and practical reason and this expresses itself vividly in his discussions of the body/mind dualism inherited from Descartes and others. Kant develops a tension between two aspects of human wholeness represented by the empirical self which is subsumed under natural necessity and the noumenal or transcendental self which is free from mechanistic nature. It is in the latter aspect of human selfhood that the affirmation of value, of moral direction, and of some of the other excluded areas of the theoretical reason, are affirmed.

The free or transcendental self of the practical sphere achieves its integration through its autonomy, and such autonomy results from the categorical imperative which becomes the integrating center for the self. What does this word "autonomy" mean in Kant's usage?

Kant was not himself clear on the question. Of course the word means, "the law of the self." But what law and which self? Is the law restricted to each individual self? But, then, are there as many laws as there are selves? Is the law, therefore, universal in character? Is there one law for the many selves? Is this law impersonal, or is it the universal law of a universal self? It is obvious that Kant had difficulties synthesizing abstract universality with vivid immediacy in his moral philosophy, and it is probably correct to say that he never satisfactorily answered these questions. This ambiguity resulted in projected answers by his successors.

The only answer which he gives is in terms of a rational faith. In this connection knowledge of God is not theoretical but practical. Its purpose is to promote morality and it must therefore be based on a consciousness of duty. The validity of the belief cannot be separated from the personal, moral attitude toward life and reality. Kant explains it: "Admitting that the pure moral law inexorably binds every man as a command (not as a rule of prudence) the righteous man may say: I will that there be a God...; I firmly abide by this, and will not let this faith be taken from me; for in this instance alone my interest, because I must not relax anything of it, inevitably determines my judgment."[19] In order to maintain the integrity of the moral law and the duty which issues from it, the human self is constrained to will the existence of God as the guarantor of the moral law; God's existence is rationally necessary. In this respect Kant insists that the source of faith is in the rational faculty of the pure practical reason. This is not a theoretical source, but it is a rational source. Practical reason is superior to theoretical reason, and from this superior reason comes rational faith. Rational faith is thus the integrating factor between mechanistic nature and moral freedom, and has its origin in morality and the practical reason. The Pascalian heart which had vetoed the mechanistic nature is transformed by Kant into the practical reason, and his solution to the impasse reflects to a great extent the coldness of the natural necessity it is supposed to transcend.

The ambiguity in Kant's philosophy concerning the meaning of autonomy resulted in a number of answers by his successors. In Fichte, Schelling and Hegel an attempt to equate "the law" with universality, and a universal self or ego, begins. Fichte introduces a view of wholeness, an absolute ego or self, derived from Kant's practical sphere, and "the law" becomes indeed the expression of such an abstract ego. Schelling, in one of his systems, projects an Absolute Nature, but this nature encompasses more than the reigning mechanism; it is similar to a kind of universal organism and thus includes aesthetic elements within it. Furthermore, Hegel attempted to bring together the Absolute Nature of

Schelling and the Absolute Ego of Fichte in his grandiose speculative experiment. Hegel's concrete universal, the Absolute Spirit, is indeed a synthesis of ultimacy and immediacy, of universality and individuality, and yet as "concrete" it comes across fundamentally as an abstraction, or as too much the incarnation of the "spirit" of the German Culture.

The response of Soren Kierkegaard to the Hegelian synthesis was more intense and hostile than Pascal's veto of Descartes. Kierkegaard viewed the Hegelian system as a vast conceptual mansion with every advantage except that human beings could not live in it. He resisted gigantic speculative adventures which contributed more and more to the negation of human personhood. As social structures tended increasingly to transform persons into mere expressions of group will, so speculative substitutes for a vibrant faith tended to have a similar effect.

Human beings were, for Kierkegaard, both free and finite. The antinomy, finitude/infinitude, which he develops in The Sickness Unto Death, expresses this ambiguity: human beings are finite, and yet not equipped for finitude. Thus infinitude arises in polar tension with the finite. In classical theological parlance, if this tension is negated by a flight into infinity then it results in the sin of pride. If there is a lapse into finitude, then, it results in the sin of concupiscence or sensuality. Each of these sins is a reflecton of the other. Moreover, they are compounded indefinitely when expressed as corporate or societal pride. It is precisely in the refusal to accept finitude and the flight into fantasy, into absolutism, which accompanies this, that nature as the finite dimension is transformed into a resource for human pride. Thus the source of the self's fulness, albeit a false-fulness, comes from the rape of finitude. In its pride the infinitely empty self fills itself, pulls into itself, the finite. This is concupiscence. The variety of ways this can compound itself is expressed by Kierkegaard under the category of human sinfulness.

In his affirmation of the tension between the finite and the infinite Kierkegaard articulates a stance of healthy anxiety, the kind of posture which leads to more authentic and gentle human beings. This image of human life functioning in the tension between finitude and infinitude, between what is and what is not, between what has been and what can or may be, sets the stage for a more dynamic view of human selfhood and tends to negate the old substance theory of the body/mind dualism. It is also a rediscovery of Pascal's assertion that the human being hovers between angel and brute, and that human nature consists of motion, whereas complete rest is death.

As Pascal saw human possibility arising through such a tension, and as he recognized that human life must be anchored in the nurturing and redemptive presence of God's revelation in Jesus of Nazareth, so also Kierkegaard understood quite well that without a transcendent center for human life, an Archimedean point, the finitude/infinitude tension would be destroyed and result in the worst forms of pride and concupiscence. Kierkegaard found this center in the Moment before God where in the figure of Jesus of Nazareth ultimacy is wedded to vivid immediacy. Without such a center, it is a short distance to the trans- moral conscience gone mad, to the beyond good and evil posture of despots and tyrants such as Hitler and Stalin.

Much of Kierkegaard's thought concerning anxiety and the finitude/infinitude tension is derived from Hegel, but in Hegel metaphysical speculation triumphs over human brokenness, while in Kierkegaard it is the divine omnipotence alone that can perform the healing and centering of human beings in their brokenness by embracing them in love, and by forgiving them in fact.

And yet our fundamental problem surfaces again in Kierkegaard. In the person who resisted the Hegelian system because of its violent effects on the human individual, we find the worst vices of such a system being consecrated by extrapolating them into the living God. Kierkegaard's concept of God as the Archimedean point for the centering of human selfhood is absolutely unmoved and immutable like the concept of Aristotle's God. Richard Kroner explains:

> Kierkegaard too seems to be convinced that the perfection of God excludes any differentiation or division. Beyond all contradictions and beyond all paradoxes God dwells on an inaccessible throne. In his eternal essence being and thought are not separated. The opposition of the finite and the infinite is completely extinguished in his infinity.[20]

In contrast to this resurfacing of the Aristotelian god in Kierkegaard's thought, a kind of union of philosophical principle with the Imperial Caesar resulting in the equation of authority with coercion, is the God revealed in Jesus of Nazareth:

> the God which the Biblical man knows participates in the inner conflicts and imperfections of the earthy world; he turns to man the sinner, warning and consoling him, protecting and punishing him; he sends him into the desert of despair and exiles him from Paradise, but ultimately he redeems the repentant sinner and raises him up to himself. [21]

This is not to minimize the important contribution that both Hegel and Kierkegaard have made to the deepening of our understanding of human selfhood. Kierkegaard uncovered much that was later to be articulated in depth psychology; through his own agonizing analyses of himself, he penetrated beyond the clarity and distinctness of Cartesian consciousness into a vast reservoir of possibility for personhood. Paradoxically, however, he was never himself healed by this self analysis. Until the end of his life he remained shut up in himself, found it very difficult to have an authentic personal relationship with another human being, and went to his death bitterly attacking the institution of the church. It was almost as though "the human thought which thinks itself in splendid isolation," the Cartesian res cogitans, had broken out of its distortion as static substance, and had begun to relate to itself dynamically, but was unable to break completely from the bondage of the Cartesian prison.

Finally, Kierkegaard's Biblical faith, an expression of his liberation insofar as this had occurred, was itself distorted by an almost unconscious identification of the God revealed in Jesus of Nazareth with a philosophical absolute remote from the vivid feeling implicit in a faith in the God of Love. To the end, Kierkegaard tended to remain a tormented incarnation of such a view of deity.

This same kind of impasse can be seen in a number of Kierkegaard's successors in twentieth century existential thought. In the early Heidegger's reflection a secularization of Christian faith takes place. The Cross of Christ is transformed into Death itself, and Death confronts Dasein, human being, with its authenticity. If human being does not accept or discover the possibility implicit in contemplating its own death, then it remains inauthentic and spurious. Here again great insights have been provided into the dynamics of human selfhood. However, at least in his early philosophy, Heidegger finds himself shut up in his own authenticity, a kind of existential self which contemplates its death in splendid isolation.

On the other hand, Sartre in his initial stage of development seems to repeat the Cartesian dualism of thought and extension by a dualism of being-for-itself and being-in-itself. The "for-itself" is human life which resists becoming an "in-itself," and through this resistance and struggle, whatever value or meaning there may be is created out of the "for-itself" in its defiance of the "in-itself." In the end, the human being ("for-itself") capitulates in death to the inexorable necessity of the static "being-in-itself." In Sartre's perspective the dualism extends, therefore, to a dichotomy between creation and redemption, or being and value. Whatever worth a person achieves comes from defiance of what is. Being and worth are not ultimately identified.

Kierkegaard, Heidegger, and Sartre have all had difficulties with relating the discovery of the dynamic self to others, and to nature, and the dualism with which we began continues to persist. These thinkers have contributed a great deal, however, to the liberation of human beings from the Cartesian reductionism, and they have also served as an antidote to those who continue the reduction by treating human existence as only an expression of the behavior of the human machine. [22]

The contribution of Martin Buber has built on the insights of Kierkegaard and others and has developed a view of intersubjectivity which breaks down the barriers between self and self, and sets up the

21

possibility of a dynamic relationship between selves. A mechanistic reaction to other human beings or to nature Buber calls an I-It relationship. This is pervasive and not totally to be dispelled. An intersubjective relationship, two subjects confronting one another, Buber calls an I-Thou relation, and this is the affirmation of a persona dimension lost in the seventeenth century dualism.

In I and Thou Buber states that the more I approach other human beings as Thou, and not It, the more they become something unique and defy objective classification. They become persons. In this respect the body of an individual person becomes a symbol for that person. I mediates the presence of that person's reality to me, participates in that reality, but does not exhaust in any way the reality of the person whose presence it mediates. It is Buber's contention that the more I am confronted by the uniqueness of this personal dimension, the more accept other persons as Thou, and in an almost incredible manner, I begin to approach the world around me (nature) also as a Thou. The more I am reconciled to other persons, the more I can achieve a sensitivity to the wonder of the world in which I live. The world no longer appears as an objective possibility for my exploitation but becomes a potentiality of mediating to me a presence through itself. It becomes a possible sacramental medium for the mediation of ultimate reality.

Buber's affirmation of dynamic selfhood is expressed in relation to other selves, to nature, and to God. It is his contention that the stronger the I of the primary word I-Thou is, the more personal is the human being. Human being is not fundamentally the reduced thought which thinks itself, nor is it merely the behavior patterns of the human machine, nor is it the existential self in splendid isolation. Its inner strength is enhanced by its ability to relate to other selves, to nature and to God. He utilizes three historical figures, Socrates, Goethe, and Jesus, as symbols for such relationships. [23]

Buber sees in the impressive self of Socrates the I of endless dialogue, an I lived continuously in a relation with other human being which is bodied forth in dialogue. Socrates never ceased to believe in the reality of other human beings and sought them out in order to meet them. He took his stand with other persons in reality, and he was no forsaken by reality. He is the model for the dialogic relation of self to self, of person to person, of a human being to other human beings.

The relationship to nature expresses itself uniquely in the self or of Goethe. Goethe's self, Buber believes, is the I of pure intercourse with nature. "Nature gives herself to it and speaks unceasingly with it revealing her mysteries to it but not betraying her mystery."[24] Goethe is the model of such a relation to nature; nature in its wholneess as a medium for the presence of the ultimate.

The remarkable Jewish saint articulates the unconditional dialogic relation of human beings to God by his response to the Galilean vision of humility revealed in Jesus of Nazareth. He states:

> how powerful even to being overpowering, and how legitimate, even to being self-evident, is the saying of I by Jesus. For it is the I of unconditional relation in which the man calls his Thou Father in such a way that he himself is simply Son....If separation ever touches him, his solidarity of relation is the greater; he speaks to others only out of this solidarity. It is useless to seek to limit this I to a power in itself or this Thou to something dwelling in ourselves.[25]

The power, Buber speaks about, is the unconditional relation itself. In such a relationship in Jesus the loving Father expresses himself in the tender elements which slowly and quietly operate by love. Jesus of Nazareth is the model for the unconditional relation between human beings and God, and as such dispels the vices of imperial ruler and ruthless moralist from the image of fatherhood -- here masculine and feminine aspects tend to unite.

Through the discovery of a dynamic selfhood by existentialist thinkers, we are finally led to the realization of the possibility that human feeling, human sensitivity, human warmth, may be something expressive of more than the merely human dimension. Perhaps such feeling may be implicit in the various levels of nature organized in different ways. And perhaps nature, which was reduced to an abstract, quantifiable mechanism, may come in its newly perceived wholeness to express levels of being and feeling lost to us since the seventeenth century. It may become once again a sacrament of the divine presence.

In conclusion, the negation of the Cartesian dualism by recent thought and the recognition of an intersubjective dynamic in which persons with relative freedom may participate points in the direction of that kind of human community mentioned earlier -- a community in which a mutual interdependence can be affirmed without pathological dependence, and without the reduction or loss of individual personhood in the process. In fact such human community can be the medium both for nurture and liberation. In the Cartesian dualism alienation of human beings from nature and from one another was the disastrous result. This alienation also worked itself out in such a way that structures of authority themselves became alienated and thus were transformed into various kinds of organized coercion, resulting in the depersonalizing of human existence and the exploitation of nature.

NOTES: Chapter Two.

1.   Alfred North Whitehead, Process and Reality (New York: The Free Press, 1957), pp. 404-408.

2.   Ibid., p. 520.

3.   See my article, "The American Death of God Theology," Anglican Theological Review, Vol. XLIX, No. 1, January, 1967, pp. 70-89. Also my article, "Urheber der heutigen 'Tod-Gottes-Theologie,'" Theologie der Gegenwart, 10 Jg. 1967, Heft 4, pp. 189-195.

4.   Thomas J.J. Altizer, The Gospel of Christian Atheism (Philadelphia: The Westminster Press, 1966), pp. 92-101.

5.   Ideally, they should also be seen as masculine traits of ultimacy, but the overpowering despotic imagery tied up with masculinity has tended to develop a cloud over this possibility.

6.   Whitehead, op. cit., p. 408.

7.   See Floyd W. Matson, The Broken Image. Man, Science and Society (New York: Doubleday and Company, 1964).

8.   See Basil Willey, The Seventeenth Century Background (Garden City: Doubleday and Company, 1953), pp. 92-97. Here Willey discusses T.S.   Eliot's phrase "the dissociation of sensibility" in regard to the Cartesian influence upon poetry. "Instead of being able, like Donne or Browne, to think and feel simultaneously, either in verse or in prose, you were now expected to think prosaically and to feel poetically." (p. 93)

9.   See Ronald V. Sampson, The Psychology of Power (New York: Pantheon Books, 1966).

10.   See Hannah Arendt, The Origins of Totalitarianism (New York: Meridian Books, 1958).

11.   Blaise Pascal, Pensees (New York: Modern Library, 1941), #277, p. 95. Used by permission of the publisher.

12.   Ibid., #358, p. 118.

13.   Ibid., #129, p. 46.

14.   Ibid., #503, p. 164.

15.   Ibid., #278, p. 95.

16.   This is not to imply that the notion of a "tenderness which loses nothing that can be saved" is exclusively Christian. The Old Testament is rich in proclamations of the motherly compassion of God.   See Deuteromony 30: 10.   Furthermore, it is particularly the suffering who are the objects of God's love.   See Psalm 34: 18, Isaiah 66:2 and Isaiah 45:22.

17.   Pascal, op. cit., #555, p. 182. Used by permission.

18.   Some of the material here discussed is based on my article, "Philosophical Megalomania," Theology and Life, Vol. 9, No. 2, Summer, 1966, pp. 146-159.

19.   Quoted by Richard Kroner in The Primacy of Faith (New York: The Macmillan Company, 1943), p. 47.   See also my article, "Rational Faith in Kant's philosophy," Anglican Theological Review, Vol. XLIII, No. 2, April, 1961, pp. 178-155.

20.   Richard Kroner, "Kierkegaard's Understanding of Hegel," Union Seminary Quarterly Review, Vol. XXI, No. 2, Part 2, January, 1966, p. 240.

21.   Ibid.

22.   Matson, op. cit. Here the reduction of a human being to a homo ex machina is seen to persist from Descartes in the seventeenth century to B.F. Skinner in the twentieth century.

23.   Martin Buber, I and Thou. Trans. by Ronald Gregor Smith. (New York: Charles Scribner's Sons, 1955), pp. 66-67.

24.   Ibid., p. 66.

25.   Ibid., p. 67.

CHAPTER THREE

AUTHORITY AND CONCEPTS OF NATURE

One of the difficulties which we face in coming to grips with a Christian understanding of authority is how to develop a view of nature which does justice to our concern for a healthy freedom and the affirmation of a nurturing and liberating presence. In the past nature conceived as a quantifiable mechanism has fostered many distortions and has resulted in the alienation of human beings from the matrices of nature.

The possibility of a transition from nature as a quantifiable mechanism to a perspective more in line with the conclusions drawn in the last chapter can certainly be seen in the concept of nature developed by Hegel. He anticipates much of what is later articulated by Alfred North Whitehead and his process view, but even so the Hegelian theory is never able to rid itself entirely of the Cartesian dualism. Consequently, "the whole Hegelian theory of nature is rent by a dualism which in the long run breaks it to pieces."[1] One aspect of this dualism was the conception of nature as a machine, a moving heap of inert material particles; the other aspect is seen in the cosmological implications of his own thought which finds that all reality is permeated by process and activity. As R.G. Collingwood suggests, "nature cannot be a mere machine, because it has in it the power to evolve out of itself, by a logicial necessity, life and mind."[2] Apparently an idea of evolution is implicit in Hegel's thought but the reigning physics made it impossible for him to develop these possibilties, as earlier it had thwarted Kant and later Marx and Engels.

It is, of course, with Darwin's theory of organic descent and the development of certain laws relative to this concept that the beginnings of a breakthrough may be seen. Organic descent has two factors implicit in it; an inner creative factor called variation, which works spontaneously and mysteriously within organisms, and an external factor, natural selection, which operates selectively on these slight variations, weeding out organisms not suitable to the environment.[3] Darwin, however, placed primary emphasis on the factor of natural selection, the external aspect, and thus, instead of breaking the power of the mechanistic world view, tended to reinforce it. He saw natural selection working externally on the organism as the true cause of the organic changes in nature. Consequently, evolution was seen initially as a description of the mechanics of organic development. As a result of this,

> The difficult part of the theory, the aspect of it which even to Darwin had remained a mystery, the inner creative factor of variation, was ignored while Darwinism was in the

course of being generally accepted, and accepted in the mechanical sense.[4]

A long history of interpretation has occurred from Darwinian views of evolution to the twentieth century concepts of certain emergent evolutionists. A common contrast during this time has often been made between Darwin and Lamarck, between emphasis upon external and internal factors in evolution. As Bernard Meland describes:

> Lamarck was supposed to have ascribed to the internal condition of the organism itself...a good deal of the initiative in the variations observed. Thus evolution could be said to be inherent in the organisms of life themselves...the decisive thrust of evolutionary change was internal process of a sort.[5]

But unfortunately, Darwin had mechanized the process, emphasizing external factors.

In the twentieth century a distinguished group of emergent evolutionists attempted to heal this impasse. Among the most notable were Henri Bergson, Conwy Lloyd-Morgan, Jan Christiaan Smuts, Samuel Alexander, and the Jesuit scientist, Pierre Teilhard de Chardin. The point of view which best articulates the stance of such emergent evolutionists is

> neither internal nor external, but a subtle interplay of both aspects; but this can make sense only if one takes into account the whole discussion of form and structure which has dominated the holistic thinking of those who speak of emergence and field theory.[6]

One of the least known and yet perhaps ablest of this group of emergent evolutionists is Jan Christiaan Smuts. His holistic perspective, similar in many ways to Lloyd-Morgan's,[7] attempts to heal the breach between matter and mind found in Cartesian dualism. He envisages a reality in which the interdependence between internal and external factors is noted, and this results in a healthy wholeness missing in the earlier views of evolution, particularly those expressed by the Darwinians.

Smuts sees a dynamic emergence of life from matter, and mind from life, and thus fills in the abyss between matter and mind fostered by Descartes. In Descartes' view the most primitive forms of life had to be a mystery since dualism offered no possible way of accounting for them. Smuts posits the emergence of life from matter, mind from life, personality from mind, and from personality the human cultural exertion which produces the life nurturing structures of society. Evolution is the emergence of wholes. For example, "a mechanistic system is one where the parts maintain their identity and thus produce their effects individually, and predictably, but that where holistic factors appear, something new and non-mechanical is introduced."[8] In Smuts' perspective every object, every concept, has a series of complex relations with its neighbors in which it interpenetrates them. As Edmund Sinnot observes: "None can be understandable outside its environment, its context. All things interact. Each is a 'field' that influences neighboring ones."[9]

This kind of emphasis on dynamic equilibrium, developed initially in the revolution in physics, makes possible a healing of the earlier discontinuities between matter and life, mind and personality. Each continues with a certain distinctness. Dead matter is obviously not organic matter, and yet, dead matter is "dead" because of the way it is formed or structured, and not because it participates in an isolated and alienated realm of being referred to as dead, inert, inorganic, or res extensa. As Smuts observes:

The difference between them (matter and life) is merely a difference in the character of their activities. So far from matter being pure inertia or passivity, it is in reality a mass of seething, palpitating energies and activities. Its very dead-weight simply means the push of inner activities...Matter itself is nothing but concentrated structural energy, energy stereotyped into structure.[10]

Consequently, this is not the merger in a simplistic manner of matter into life, a kind of vitalism, but the recognition that what human beings perceive as inert matter is actually energy stereotyped into structure. The error arises when such perceptual stereotypes are taken to be the fundamental models for all levels of nature. Such an equation, Whitehead has called, "the fallacy of misplaced concreteness."[11]

This dynamic view of matter is not alienated from life as the earlier concept was. In fact it affirms that matter approximates to life. Matter is not life, but implicit in the form and structure (the external factor) of matter is the energy which approximates to life (the internal factor). As a result of this, "the structure of matter is also in a sense creative -- creative, that is to say, not of its own stuff, but of the forms, arrangements and patterns which constitute all its value in the physical sphere."[12]

Smuts insists in his holistic approach that value is not something dissociated or alienated from physical reality, but rather that the source of value is implicit in such reality. The values that arise from structures of life, mind, personality, and culture are peculiar to those structures. Values, peculiar to physical structures, also inhere in such forms. He recognizes that "in a very real sense the idea of value applies as truly and effectively in the domain of the physical as in that of the biological or psychical. In both cases value is a quality of the forms and combinations which are brought about."[13] Consequently, Smuts would not be uncomfortable with Pascal's "we feel it in a thousand things," or with Buber's understanding of nature as a potential Thou in intersubjective relationships.

A great deal more can be said of Smuts' important contribution. As we have seen he traces his theory of emergence through all the various levels of matter, life, mind, personality, and culture. But the distinctive contribution here emphasized is in his articulation of the interdependence between external and internal factors, his affirmation of an inner creativity in the evolutionary process, and his recognition that a quantifiable mechanism is a distortion of this holistic vision, that the forms and structures of nature (quantity) are not isolated or alienated from the energy or activity (internal factors) stereotyped by them. A unity of fact and value is affirmed, a unity of quantity and quality. Loren Eiseley sums it up: "Evolution, if it has taught us anything, has taught us that life is infinitely creative."[14]

The vision of Jan Smuts is a vision we need to take seriously today. The inner creative thrust of the evolutionary process, he affirms, as leading towards wholeness, healing, holiness. Such affirmations are more in the area of faith statements, reflecting a conviction that the world or universe is ultimately a benevolent place, where fact and value unite. It is as though "the field of nature...is the source of the grand ecology of the universe. It is the environment, the Society -- vital, friendly, educative, creative -- of all wholes and all souls."[15] It is, indeed, ultimately nurturing and redemptive.

While Smuts and the emergent evolutionists were attempting to heal the wounds caused by the violence of the mechanistic reduction of nature and human being, Alfred North Whitehead was also approaching this impasse from another point of view, one which was fundamentally in harmony with the intentions of the evolutionists.

Whitehead was a mathematician like Pascal, who in his later years turned to philosophy, constructing a speculative cosmology which was a reflection of his commitment to restructure the human vision of reality in a more holistic and organismic direction. It might be accurate to say that he did for modern physics what Smuts and the other emergent evolutionists did for biology. He injected both a within and a without, an external and an internal factor, or as he would say, a physical and a mental pole, into the fundamental things which go to make up the dynamic reality in which we participate and with which we are confronted.

Smuts rejected the concept of inert matter, and found that the inertness is actually energy stereotyped into structure. What we perceive on the human level are precisely such stereotypes, and if these stereotypes or objects of human perception become the models for all reality, then a fundamental distortion occurs. When sticks and stones, or any other object of human perception, are seen as the fundamental things in reality, this results in the predominance of static or substance views of nature. It comes, as a result, of the pretension of human beings assuming that their conscious perspective is definitive for all that is the case. Even so, "consciousness is only the last and greatest of such elements by which the selective character of the individual obscures the external totality from which it originates and which it embodies."16

One of Whitehead's fundamental tasks was the placing of human perception in the context of a totality or wholeness of being and meaning which transcended the human perceptual bias and yet at the same time acknowledged its proper character and function. The only way a human being can fulfill such an obligation is through the creative use of the imagination and through, in the best sense of the expression, a speculative reconstruction leading up to and including the dimensions of reality shaped and ordered by the human perceptual process. As the data for modern physics are not sensible data derived from human perception, but rather intellectual constructions which account for what is lost in human perception, so Whitehead engages in a similar project, a reconstruction which more effectively includes dimensions lost in past reductions based on faulty perceptual views. Pascal's vast reservoir of possibility, symbolized by the heart, and his "we feel it in a thousand things," are included in Whitehead's speculative reconstruction.

The explication of Whitehead's views, even when reduced to a minimal simplicity, is on first reading usually considered to be exceedingly complex. The following discussion may also be judged in that manner. Its intention, however, is to describe a new way of envisioning reality, which can then serve as a liberating instrument in expelling past abstractions; abstractions which still constitute the unconscious structure through which we view reality. To displace such a structure is itself a highly complex task.

When deliberating upon the discussion that follows, a number of points need to be kept in mind. First, Whitehead is developing a new conceptuality which may appear to be strange on first impression; it is a conceptuality which has to be gradually felt as well as thought. It must be absorbed into the total self so that the other unconscious structure can be displaced. Secondly, the first several pages of description will be dealing with reality below the level of human consciousness, a kind of speculative description of microcosmic reality as contrasted with the clear and distinct macrocosmic reality of human perception. This is necessary in order to avoid the pitfalls we have already encountered in the fallacy of misplaced concreteness. Thirdly, a clear and distinct understanding of this microcosmic reality should not be expected on first reading. Here we are dealing with matters of feeling, with matters of the heart, with visceral as opposed to cerebral feeling, but we are expressing it by necessity in a cerebral manner. Although poets, artists, and musicians often convey this reality more poignantly, it is Whitehead's contention that even in the most primitive feeling there is both a mental and a physical aspect, and what differentiates the various levels of reality, matter, life, mind, etc., are the particular ways this feeling is organized or structured. Fourthly, Whitehead's feeling, or what he also calls prehensive activity, which persists below the level of human consciousness and human perception, is an attempt to unite quantity and quality, fact and value, so that the energy or activity described by modern physics may be envisioned as vibrant feeling, and the so-called vector transmission of energy in physics is transformed into a vector transmission of feeling.

It may be said that Whitehead's philosophy is a philosophy of feeling, a speculative description which accounts for all the varieties of feeling; conformal, conceptual, comparative, propositional, intellectual; and which finds that human consciousness presupposes such a vast reservoir of emotion. So, in what follows, it will be necessary to launch into the deep, and if the first net comes up empty, keep casting! Gradually an abundance of insights should emerge from the vastness of the deep, that presupposed reservoir of feeling which until recently was dissociated from conceptual activity.

When an attempt is made to restructure reality which escapes human perception since human perception presupposes it, the popular tendency is to treat such speculative or intellectual constructions as though they were minute perceptual objects. This is a fundamental error. For example, the concept of electrons and protons was developed in modern physics in order to account for a mass of seething, palpitating energies and activities. Electrons and protons are not microscopic or sub-microscopic objects. The physicist does not perceive electrons and protons; he constructs them as ways of accounting for what he is able to perceive.

It is also difficult to understand an explanation of so-called unconscious processes from the viewpoint of a clear and distinct conscious perspective. Perhaps a few examples will be helpful in achieving this. The vast activity which goes on in a particular human body is for the most part unnoticed. It is presupposed by conscious actions, but is not actually within the conscious perspective of the particular person in question. The fact that the body is made up of a multiplicity of complex organs working together in a dynamic equilibrium and interdependence is taken for granted. We perceive some of these organs, the eyes, for example; but we do not perceive the eye seeing something. We perceive another person's eye as one organ in that person's body, or we may perceive our own eyes in a mirror, but what we confront is an external organ, complex in its make-up, and a part of the total human organism. The eye sees, nevertheless; and although we do not perceive the eye seeing, we do feel it and such a statement makes sense. It is this inner working of the eye that we feel, and this kind of activity is analogous to the prehensive activity or feeling which Whitehead posits. Another example can be drawn from the experience of gradually coming into consciousness after the anesthesia wears off after an operation. The vast organismic activity of the human body has been going on up to that point, but there has been no awareness at all. Then there are a few flickerings of consciousness, yet still characterized by a certain vagueness and dimness. Finally, one recovers the clarity and distinctness of human consciousness. This illustrates what Whitehead meant when he declared that consciousness is only the last and greatest of such elements by which the selective character of the individual obscures the external totality from which it originates and which it embodies. If we were to use the human body as a model for the totality of reality, then perhaps some hints are achieved as to how one can reconstruct reality below the level of consciousness. One final way this becomes poignant to us is when we suffer severe pain in some part of the body. The pain calls attention to a disturbance in the bodily equilibrium, and makes us consciously concentrate on an area of the body which otherwise would probably be taken for granted. Fundamental to Whitehead's reconstruction, consequently, is the recognition of this vast prehensive activity. He insists upon the primacy of such feeling

In Whitehead's view of reality, the actual entity, or actual occasion of experience, is the res vera, the true thing or reality. But Whitehead's actual occasions a re not minute, microscopic particles, but speculative reconstructions comparable to electrons and protons in modern physics. Moreover, a process occurs in the origination of each actual occasion. A multiplicity of feelings, through a selective activity in relation to the past, comes together to form an actual occasion. Many feelings concresce (come together) in order to become an actual occasion, a drop of experience. It is obvious from this explanation that there are not first actual occasions which undergo qualifications and modifications, a substance/accidents model; but rather many feelings come together (this process is itself a kind of subject), and from this process arises an actual occasion, a feeling-unit, a drop of experience, and the emergent actual occasion is a superject. As a result, we are dealing here with a subject/superject model. At the point when the coming together (concrescence) is complete then the superject or actual occasion perishes and becomes objectively immortal; it becomes itself a datum for future prehensive activity or feeling, as a new occasion feels it as a part of the past, and so on. It is difficult to give an example of this, but perhaps a split-second of human experience in its relation to the immediately past split-second of experience might serve as an analogy to certain kinds of actual occasions. Furthermore, past fact and future possibility is maintained, and a breakthrough into novelty may occur.

It is at this point that Whitehead is able to account for the emergence of life from matter, to use Smuts' language. Matter is primarily conformal feeling, but feeling nevertheless; life, however, comes when the contrast is discovered between the was and the may be. Consequently, the famous finitude/infinitude tension which Kierkegaard rightly regarded as being fundamental to human reality is extrapolated by Whitehead into a tension between conformal feeling (finitude) and the emergence of the contrast (infinitude) into the elemental difference between matter and life, the inorganic and the organic. He says: "The characteristic of life is reaction adapted to the capture of intensity under a large variety of circumstances. But the reaction is dictated by the present and not by the past. It is the clutch at vivid immediacy."[17]

Life for Whitehead is a bid for freedom, a breakthrough from the conformity to the past (conformal feeling, matter) into the contrast between what has been and what may become the case. "Life is the name for originality, and not for tradition."[18]

As the possibility for novelty arises, the eternal objects are felt more and more as transcendent, pried loose from their immanence in past actual occasions; and as transcendent, they become possibilities for creative breakthrough and novelty. From the simple comparative feelings which account for the emergence of life, complex comparative feelings arise, feelings which contrast conceptual possibility with physical feelings, and such comparisons may develop into propositions where the physical feelings become less distinct and prominent, and the conceptual feelings become more intense and dominant. When such propositions are felt, this is the point where consciousness emerges, both animal and human. As Whitehead has stated, "consciousness presupposes experience,"[19] and such unconscious experience is the vast prehensive activity or feeling we have been describing; consciousness is the tip of the experiential iceberg.

Through this very brief and sketchy account of prehensive activity or feeling, we have reached the point where human perception, as contrasted with prehensive activity, occurs. As Smuts considered objects of human perception to be energy stereotyped into structures, so Whitehead understands such objects of preception to be societies and nexūs (plural of nexus) of actual occasions. What the human being perceives in a simple object, a stone for example, is a multiplicity of actual occasions, organized in a kind of social order which perseveres as a stone, energy stereotyped into structure.

The social order which occurs that accounts for the vast multiplicity of perceptual objects, whether they be sticks and stones, plants and animals, manufactured things or human beings, ranges from simple

34

to complex, from one society to a society of societies and nexūs. All these perceptual objects, however, are primarily organized prehensive activity or feeling, a multiplicity of drops of experience, actual occasions or entities, perceived as objects in the classical sense of that word. As we discussed previously, at the point where animal and human consciousness arises, complex comparative feelings, or intellectual feelings, or propositional feelings, express themselves in relation to such contrasts and complexity in the immediate past. At the point of human consciousness conceptual possibilities in the form of propositional feeling become clear and distinct and the physical feelings to which they are contrasted become dim and vague; as a result, prehensive activity or feeling is thus organized and pulled together by some eternal objects (forms of possibility) such as color, hardness or softness, shape, etc., and these latter conceptual aspects dominate. Furthermore, what emerges is the clear and distinct perceptual object, the tip of the experiential iceberg, from the vastness of the presupposed prehensive activity or feeling, now dim and vague.

The clarity and distinctness of the perceptual object is the point where Descartes began his philosophical dichotomy. He abstracted this clear and distinct idea (perceptual object) from the prehensive activity or feeling from which it had arisen and came up with an extended thing (res extensa). Such an abstraction is perception as presentational immediacy, and when divorced from the presupposed prehensive activity or feeling (perception as causal efficacy), it distorts what is the case; it is the fallacy of misplaced concreteness.

Whitehead unites these two important aspects of human perceptual activity, causal efficacy (prehensive activity), and presentational immediacy (the clear and distinct idea abstracted from its causal past), into a theory of perception as symbolic reference. This is a mixed mode in which the feeling tone of the presupposed prehensive activity is synthesized with the clear and distinct idea, and this mixed mode rescues from vagueness and dimness a contemporary spatial region. The human perceiver projects such a mixed mode on to the spatial region, thus injecting the full feeling tone of the prehensive activity into the human perceptual object. Thus Pascal's "we feel it in a thousand things," is confirmed by Whitehead's view of human perception, while it stands in contrast to the Cartesian and mechanistic distortions of human perceptual activity.

Whitehead also rejects the Cartesian dualism between body and mind by an affirmation of the psychosomatic unity of the human person. The human body is a complex society of societies, both living and non-living; a complexity of healthy wholeness and dynamic equilibrium, presided over by an actual occasion, which can be called the human soul or person. He says concerning such a presiding occasion:

each actual occasion has a physical pole and a mental pole, and as a datum, offers what has been structured through its own distinctive character or subjective form to the occasions in process of becoming.

Prehensive activity as it responds to the immediate past is primarily or basically conformal in character. One type of organized feeling is, then, conformal feeling to the data of the immediate past. Its conformity, however, does not take away from its distinctness as an occasion of experience; in this respect, each occasion is unique. The conformity is best understood as a response to the past, and a reproduction of the past with a bare minimum of such distinctness resulting.

In the above description the feeling of the past has primarily emphasized the so-called physical pole of past occasions. A mental pole, however, is also present in every past actual occasion. This brings us to the second important element in his reconstruction of reality. This is the element of continuing possibility, which Whitehead refers to as eternal objects.

Eternal objects are not the same as the old philosophic universals, although they probably come closer to them than anything else. Eternal objects represent continuing possibility, denoting other kinds of feeling than merely conformal feelings. When an eternal object is felt, such a feeling is conceptual.

In terms of our discussion conformal feeling predominates at the primary level of prehensive activity, while conceptual feelings are dim and indistinct. Nevertheless, it is precisely the eternal objects (or forms of possibility) which are immanent in an actual occasion and which give that occasion its distinctness and uniqueness. When an actual occasion emerges which is primarily conformal to its past, then, the conceptual feeling of the occasion is also in conformity to the peculiar way the past datum occasions have actualized the possibility of the eternal objects or forms immanent in them. The conceptual feeling is minimal because it is the feeling of an eternal object actualized in the past datum occasion, and not an eternal object (form of possibility) "pried loose" from the past actual occasion, so that a new possibility, or the emergence of novelty, can occur.

When such eternal objects are pried loose from their immanent location in a past actual occasion serving as a datum, then the possibility of a contrast between what was and what may be arises. In conformal feeling, the datum from the past provides the direction for the present on the basis of its own immanent eternal object, or its own possibility actualized in a peculiar way. When the contrast arises, a new direction may be discovered. If the contrast is weak, there is a lapse back into the conformal. On the other hand, if the contrast between what was and what may be is strong, then the tension between

The final percipient route of occasions is perhaps some thread of happenings wandering in 'empty space' amid the interstices of the brain. It toils not, neither does it spin. It receives from the past; it lives in the present. It is shaken by the intensities of private feeling, adversion and aversion. In its turn, this culmination of bodily life transmits itself as an element of novelty throughout the avenues of the body. Its sole use to the body is its vivid originality: it is the organ of novelty.[20]

As we have already described, actual entities or actual occasions are the true realities and eternal objects are the forms of possibility, which permit advance into novelty. In Whitehead's system all aspects of reality must be located in some sense in actual entities or actual occasions. Human perceptual objects are constituted by a multiplicity of actual occasions stereotyped into particular social structures. What about eternal objects or the forms of possibility? Are they free-floating forms of possibility? Certainly not in Whitehead's account. They must have a location. We have found them as actualized in a particular way in past actual occasions which serve as data for prehensive activity currently in process of becoming actual. Furthermore, we have described them as being "pried loose" from such immanence, as being transcendent. Where are such forms of possibility located when they are conceptually prehended or felt as transcendent, as possibilities for the actualization of novelty? Whitehead locates all the forms of possibility, the eternal objects, in a non-temporal actual entity, God.

The Whiteheadian concept of God sees God as an actual entity. "There is no going behind actual entities to find anything more real. They differ among themselves; God is an actual entity, and so is the most trivial puff of existence in far-off empty space."[21] God is a non-temporal actual entity in the sense that God does not perish as all other actual occasions do. God is rather the chief exemplification of the principle that affirms actual entities or occasions as the real things. The location of the forms of possibility does not perish thus insuring always fresh possibilities for novelty in the creative process.

Whitehead's view of God is based on the Galilean vision of humility expressed in the life and death of Jesus of Nazareth, and he builds into his metaphysical explanation such a vision of the Divine Reality. What follows as metaphysical explanation should be recognized as the attempt to explicate such a vision of God, derived from Jesus, and to use such an explanation as a basis for grasping the wholeness of being and meaning, the unity of thought and feeling, fact and value; in other words, the triumph of divine love over coercive power and its many incarnations in past history.

Whitehead's concept of God is dipolar. Two aspects of deity are delineated. The first is the primordial aspect. God "is the unconditional actuality of conceptual feeling at the base of things; so that, by reason of this primordial actuality, there is an order in the relevance of eternal objects to the process of creation."[22] God is the actual location for the forms of possibility, the eternal objects. In this sense God is the primordial instantiation of creativity, and in this instantiation is located the forms of possibility which stand for emergence of novelty in the creative process. As primordial, God is eternal. Eternal objects, forms of possibility, do not perish. Consequently, God does not perish as the location for conceptual valuation and the lure to novelty.

The second pole of God is the consequent aspect of deity. Whitehead understands God as the beginning and the end. God is the beginning in the sense that deity is "the presupposed actuality of conceptual operation, in unison of becoming with every other creative act."[23] The consequent aspect means the pole of physical feeling in God as the primordial aspect emphasized conceptual valuation and feeling. Whitehead explains:

> The completion of God's nature into a fulness of physical feeling is derived from the objectification of the world in God. He shares with every new creation its actual world; and the consequent creature is objectified in God as a novel element in God's objectification of that actual world.....God's conceptual nature is unchanged by reason of its final completion. But his derivative nature is consequent upon the creative advance of the world.[24]

All actual entities (occasions), except God, once they have achieved satisfaction, i.e., actuality, perish, and as a result become data for present and future prehensive activity. All actual occasions become objectively immortal, and find their location as immortal in the consequent nature of deity, the physical feeling pole of God. The vast creative advance, the feeling-tones of all actual occasions are conserved in the positive prehension or feeling of such realities in the everlasting or consequent nature of deity. This consequent nature of God is the judgment of God on the world. It is the judgement of a tenderness which loses nothing that can be saved, and the wisdom which uses what in the temporal world has been mere wreckage. Another way of describing this is:

> An actual entity in the temporal world is to be conceived as originated by physical experience with its process of completion motivated by consequent, conceptual experience initially derived from God. God is to be conceived as originated by conceptual experience with his process of completion motivated by consequent, physical experience, initially derived from the temporal world.[25]

These two aspects, the primordial and the consequent, constitue the dipolar nature of deity.

Another observation needs to be made. It has to do with Whitehead's concept of initial aim. Initial aim is the peculiar lure which is provided by the conceptual valuation of God and given to each actual occasion in its process of becoming actual. Such an aim may or may not be realized, but God offers for each actual occasion a vision of what that occasion may become. Such an initial aim

> constitutes the ideal of growth that would result in maximum ordered complexity in the world were it realized in fact -- this is God's mode of operation in the world, designed to produce the kind of world that, physically prehended by his consequent nature, would result in the maximum intensity of satisfaction for him.[26]

In this sense the divine love is not coercive, and through the gift of initial aim the process of an actual occasion concrescing is lured towards as full a satisfaction as is possible for that occasion given the reality at the moment, with the understanding that such an ideal may not be achieved. Such a view of divine power is often rejected because of the dominant image of the imperial ruler, the model of omnipotent, coercive, despot. But in Whitehead's reconstruction,

> God's role is not the combat of productive force with productive force, of destructive force with destructive force; it lies in the patient operation of the overpowering rationality of his conceptual harmonization. He does not create the world, he saves it.[27]

Whitehead understands such a view of the Divine Reality to be more consistent with the revelation of God in the events surrounding the life and death of Jesus of Nazareth, than the traditional image of an omnipotent, impassible, immutable, Caesar-god, who also by some trick of verbal magic, cares about the world, and loves it.

The dipolar view emphasizes that God's nature is ever enlarging itself. "In it the complete adjustment of the immediacy of joy and suffering reaches the final end of creation."[28] In the Divine Reality ultimacy is wedded to vivid immediacy, and

> the sense of worth beyond itself is immediately enjoyed as an overpowering element in individual self-attainment. It is in this way that the immediacy of sorrow and pain is transformed into an element of triumph. This is the notion of redemption through suffering which haunts the world.[29]

God is the fellow-sufferer who understands. Such a view of deity is a radical departure from past conceptions, but it is the kind of Divine Reality usually confronted in worship; a living God unsurpassable in perfection and holiness by all else, but capable of surpassing itself.[30]

As Buber's affirmation of a dynamic selfhood leads to an intersubjectivity which breaks the isolation and alienation of the Cartesian thinking thing, so Smuts, Whitehead and others have in their reconstruction in evolutionary and process thought rescued nature from mechanistic reduction and distortion, and at the same time, restored to nature the intensity of feeling, both physical and conceptual, which was lost in the seventeenth century. With Whitehead's initial aim, a kind of prevenient divine grace, serving as a lure to novelty and intensity of satisfaction, we can gain insight into the affirmation of authority as the creative and redemptive (liberating) presence of the Divine Reality, and also into the way such presence may be mediated both through nature and human beings.

In conclusion, the remarkable insights of Smuts and Whitehead into the dymanics of nature support the intersubjective dynamic of Buber, and the two views together offer an alternative to the older mechanistic perspectives on nature and human existence. These insights are also helpful in understanding organic models of human community. When nature is seen as a creative, dynamic activity in process of emergence, then an organic model of human community takes on a similar dynamic character and possibility. It is no longer understood as a kind of natural necessity from which individual freedom must be alienated, but rather is precisely the creative and nurturing matrix from which life, as the bid for freedom, arises. In this understanding, no alienation is necessary. Out of the creative and nurturing matrix of nature emerges both the dimension of personhood and also the intersubjective dynamic, and from this we are able to discern the historical drama of human life in which the various cultural spheres constituting the social fabric are operative.

NOTES: Chapter Three

1.   R.G. Collingwood, The Idea of Nature (New York: Oxford University Press, 1960), p. 128.

2.   Ibid.

3.   Jan Christiaan Smuts, Holism and Evolution (New York: The Viking Press, 1961), p. 182.

4.   Ibid., pp. 189-190. The effect of this distortion is still very much with us, particularly as it expressed itself in theories of social process known as Social Darwinism. Through natural selection, interpreted as

the survival of the fittest, the various social strata were seen to be the result of such a process, and the poor and disadvantaged were obviously in that condition because of their inferiority. This justified amassing huge wealth, exploiting nature and its resources, destroying other forms of life which could not survive such a human rape of nature, keeping the labor force impoverished since human labor was primarily only a functioning machine for the fittest to use; and now in affluent America where most of the labor force has also achieved the status of the fittest, the whole society has become a kind of producing and consuming machine, and as a result of this the desire arises to utilize the natural resources of other parts of the world in order to feed the mammoth machine we have created -- a machine which claims more and more of us as abstract functioning units. In connection with this a popular view persists that we deserve these resources because of our affluence, strength, and superiority, another aspect of Darwinian natural selection.

5.   Bernard E. Meland, "Evolution and the Imagery of Religious Thought from Darwin to Whitehead," Process Philosophy and Christian Thought, edited by Delwin Brown, Ralph E. James, Jr., and Gene Reeves (Indianapolis: Bobbs-Merrill Company, Inc., 1971), p. 422.

6.   Ibid., p. 423.

7.   Smuts, op. cit.   See also Conwy Lloyd-Morgan, Emergent Evolution (London: Williams and Norgate, 1923), and Life, Mind and Deity (London: Williams and Norgate, 1926).

8.   Edmund W. Sinnot, "Introduction to Holism and Evolution", Smuts, op. cit., p. xiii.

9.   Ibid.

10.   Smuts, op. cit., p. 51.

11.   Whitehead, op cit., p. 10

12.   Smuts, op. cit., p. 55.

13.   Ibid., p. 56.

14.   Loren Eiseley, Darwin's Century (Garden City: Doubleday and Company, 1961), p. 347.

15.   Smuts, op. cit., p. 343. In the same spirit as Smuts, Loren Eiseley muses: "I would say that if 'dead' matter has reared up this curious landscape of fiddling crickets, song sparrows, and wondering men, it must be plain even to the most devoted materialist that the matter of which he speaks contains amazing, if not dreadful powers, and may not

be, as Hardy has suggested, 'but one mask of many worn by the Great Face behind.'" The Immense Journey (New York: Vintage Books, 1961), p. 210.

16. Whitehead, op. cit., p. 18.

17. Ibid., p. 124. This description of Whitehead's cosmology is by necessity an incomplete one. For a thorough treatment, see his Process and Reality, or the helpful A Key to Whitehead's Process and Reality by Donald W. Sherburne, now published by University of Chicago Press. One of the better introductions to Whitehead's thought is Ivor LeClerc, Whitehead's Metaphysics (Bloomington: Indiana University Press, 1958).

18. Ibid., p. 124.

19. Ibid., p. 67.

20. Ibid., p. 400. In this connection a human body or an animal body is a complex society of societies directed by a presiding occasion, a kind of monarchical structure in the literal meaning of the word. In contrast to this, plants do not have such a presiding occasion in the peculiar sense that animals and human beings do. The nature of plant or vegetable life is thus more democratic, and less self-directed; yet plant and vegetable life is a complex society of actual occasions, organized prehensive activity or feeling.

21. Ibid., p. 23.

22. Ibid., p. 405.

23. Ibid., p. 406.

24. Ibid., p. 406-407.

25. Ibid., p. 407.

26. Donald W. Sherburne, A Key To Whitehead's Process and Reality (New York: The Macmillan Company, 1966), p. 244.
27. Whitehead, op. cit., p. 408.

28. Ibid., p. 412.

29. Ibid.

30. For a slightly different approach to this insight, see Charles Hartshorne, The Divine Relativity (New Haven: Yale University Press, 1948).

The concept of God as the fellow-sufferer who understands, which is also a key idea in the Old Testament, is developed by Abraham Heschel in The Prophets (New York: Harper and Row, 1962). See particularly Chapter 12, "The Theology of Pathos," pp. 221-231, and Chapter 18, "Religion of Sympathy," pp. 307-323.

CHAPTER FOUR

AUTHORITY AND CULTURE

Humankind's primary intellectual experience is linguistic. Words (or The Word) are fundamental in such experience and in the shaping of such experience. J.H. Randall, Jr. has observed: "We start all our reflection with the world already formulated in words. Aristotle puts it: we start with 'what the world is said to be,' 'with previous knowledge,' We set out, if not with 'the world known,' at least with the world already sorted out into the categories of our institutionalized language habits."[1]

It is Randall's further contention that the return to the Aristotelian concern for language as the primary intellectual experience for human beings is an improvement over the preoccupation of the early modern period with sensation and perception as the data of knowledge. When sense data arise as a result of the emergence of human consciousness, we find that consciousness has already initially articulated its apprehension of the world through institutionalized language habits present in its nurturing matrix. Language is thus primary in cultural and individual development, and, consequently, is basic when considering the question of cultural nurture and cultivation. Randall clarifies this point even more by declaring: "Linguistic formulation is not the end, or outcome of knowledge, but enters into the very 'data' of knowledge. It would doubtless be better to say, the 'prehensa,' the 'taken,' rather than the 'data,' 'the given.'"[2] As a result, the data for human knowledge are not initially sense data, but linguistic data.

Human conscious experience is formed and shaped by the words of language, and, as a result, all so-called sense data already presuppose, in addition to the vast prehensive activity already considered, the linguistic cultivation implicit in the cultural nurturing matrix. In the beginning are the words. It should be affirmed, however, that linguistic formulation is not the end nor the outcome of knowledge. It is not final. The function of language is to permit human beings to ask questions. Consequently, it is a mediate and instrumental function. Words are never an end in themselves; they rather constitute a process in which ever new horizons and dimensions of knowledge and conscious experience may open up. Randall suggests that knowing is a power to operate, a power to do something. Linguistic formulation is a means to operating and doing it. In other words knowing is ultimately the power to know how to live well.[3]

From this brief discussion we can understand what is fundamental in the process of human maturation. Culture expresses itself in a variety of linguistic forms. These data are an intimate part of what is "taken in" in the cultivation of our human selfhood. They are the foundation for the nurture of human life and thought. The "universes of discourse" which these linguistic data articulate constitute the "reality" available to us in the process of human growth and development. The cultural nurture represented by the linguistic forms presents the possibility of a cultivated experience, or feeling, or subjectivity that is enabled to grasp the objective world of reality.

This point should be developed further by considering the multiplicity of linguistic forms, not only in the sense of individual words, but also in the sense of the many universes of discourse that possess their own peculiar linguistic formulations, and their own peculiar logics. Randall has expressed the thesis that language makes a subject matter intelligible, and as a result, intelligibility is the mediate and proximate function of language. Ludwig Wittgenstein has demonstrated that there are a multiplicity of "intelligibilities" which he calls language games.[4] Randall enlarges on this when he states:

> Different "sciences," philosophies and organized bodies of ideas are thus all different schemes or systems of "intelligibility." They are many and diverse. They are all based on certain natural structures or relations, which each selects and reorganizes for its own purposes...All these schemes... function in a context that is social and historical, a context which sets the further ends of language, that is, determines the specific kind of intelligibility it is the function of these schemes to provide. That is, "intelligibility" as the mediate function of language has a more ultimate function that is socially and historically conditioned and determined.[5]

This more ultimate function of language can be found in his declaration that a universe of action and experience is the precondition for any universe of discourse. This can be illustrated as follows: A 'particular person' is born into the human situation. This situation is already highly charged with linguistic formulation, representative of a multiplicity of universes of discourse. The more cultivated the person becomes, the more, theoretically at least, he can distinguish between the universes of discourse as nurturing, conditioning, and informing agencies, on the one hand, and as limited articulations of the more basic universe of action and experience on the other. The more breakthroughs of this sort will result in more selective and purposive activity, in more critical evaluation of the given (or taken) universes of discourse. Such selectivity, critical evaluation, and purposive action can develop because the universes of discourse represented by the linguistic formulations become truly mediate, opening up the broader universe of action and experience.

It is within the realm of possibility that some persons may never make a critical breakthrough. In this event the particular universes of discourse in which they have been nurtured and conditioned are the equivalent in their experience of the universe of action and experience.

The reduced areas as articulated in linguistic forms and discourse will equal the whole of what is the case. The distinguishing mark of the human being, however, is precisely in the possibility of such break-throughs. Universes of discourse are broken, so to speak, by the enlargement of experience.

The universes of discourse are in the beginning for each of us. Cultural nurture and conditioning is the presupposition of human maturation. Yet the peculiarity of being human precludes the ultimacy of the universes of discourse and their words. The human person may rise above the nurturing and conditioning agencies of culture, and he may alter them, reform them, change them, inject new dimensions of insight into them, exert action on them. Consequently, the following healthy tension in human life and thought arises:6 Culture conditions and nurtures experience; experience initiates and creates culture. Both poles of the tension must be affirmed.

From the preceding observations, it can be concluded that authority is indeed vested in universes of discourse and their linguistic formulations. It can also be ascertained that the function of such authority as it represents the multiplicity of universes of discourse is to nurture and cultivate human beings, enabling them to become truly centered selves or persons, and thus, relatively free beings. Certainly, all human beings are dependent on cultural structures for nurture and cultivation, but at the same time, this dependence is, or should be, complemented by the relative freedom of each person so nurtured; such a state then makes the posture of human dependence relative also. This position affirms the definition of authority posited in Chapter One.

The question may arise, however, concerning societal structures, universes of discourse, cultural agencies, whatever they may be, which fail to serve as nurturing and cultivating influences an dbecome instead smothering and enslaving forces, resulting in oppression rather than relative freedom. Such structures have been designed originally to nurture but have ceased to do this, or they may have been developed to protect at all costs, or to enclose, rather than to occasion break-throughs into responsible freedom. Whenever such distortions occur, the attempt to negate the healthy tension between culture and experi-ence is obvious. This is the source for most of the negative feeling about authority today. Furthermore, resistance to such smothering, enslaving, oppressing structures should be understood not as a resis-tance to authority, but rather to a distortion of authority which may be referred to as authoritarianism. Such authoritarianism is actually coercive power masked as authority.

All authoritarianism denies the aforementioned healthy tension, and certainly negates the posited definition of authority in Chapter One. Authoritarian distortions oppress and smother through a subtle violence and coercion that destroys or attempts to destroy the human condition. In such a context Ivan Illich is correct when he says that living violence always breaks out against the demand that a person submit to idols.7 The basis for "legitimate" revolutionaly activity is centered here, since such activity is a response to authoritarian distortions, and not a negation of the authority which nurtures and cultivates human freedom.

The tension posed between culture and experience will now be enlarged. Culture conditions and nurtures experience. This has already been demonstrated when the discussion focused on the relation of universes of discourse and their linguistic formulations to the nurture of human persons. The words are indeed in the beginning of human conscious experience; in the process of development, one must first master the given or "what is taken in" by language forms before he is in a position to make a breakthrough and to a degree become an initiator of culture itself. One of the signs of a so-called educated or cultivated person (this should not be necessarily measured by formal education as the formally educated are often victimized as much by linguistic formulation as others) is the ability when the time is ripe to make the necessary breakthroughs from the matrices that have been responsible for his nurture and cultivation. When this happens, he is then liberated from what could have been a prison house of the spirit, and is free to inject new life and new forms into the cultural givens. Thus an affirmation of the other pole in the tension arises: experience initiates and creates culture.

We must now focus our attention on four spheres of cultural exertion, and upon the relation of these spheres to the question of cultural nurture and the relation of human freedom to that nurture. Involved will also be a delineation of the peculiar way that such spheres become expressions of authority. The four spheres of cultural exertion are classified by two general areas of culture: contemplation and action.8

Contemplation (theoria) as one general area expresses itself from the perspective of "world" categories. The contemplative task seeks to unite or at least to relate the many world perspectives into one world picture or focus. A manifold of worlds corresponds to the multiplicity of conscious experiences embodied in selves or persons. In a peculiar way, every conscious self or person has his own world. Contemplation is thus world oriented and focused.

Action (praxis), as the other general area, is the cultural exertion concerned with the relationship between the many selves or persons, Buber's intersubjective dynamic. If a particular person is not to make all others, things or objects, within his conscious world perspective, then a dimension of reality arises which is not focused on the world (or worlds) but rather on the interpersonal. This is undoubtedly what Randall had in mind when he declared that knowing is ultimately the power to know how to live well. Thus the presuppostion of contemplative work is the interpersonal dimension (action).

The contemplative area issues into at least two distinct cultural spheres: science and art. The peculiar function of science is the creation of a universe (or universes) of discourse in which all sense data and other evidence are subordinated to a perspective or focus, singular and/or plural, of the world. Such a task is never completed. The scientist should not become the victim of his own universes of discourse, since they should never be equated totally with the universe of action and experience. Such an equation would stifle scientific work. The future should always be open for the scientific community, and its universes of discourse subject to further modification, replacement, or critical scrutiny. A tension between the available world (what is represented to date by the universes of discourse) and the unexplored or unshaped world constitutes the posture of authentic scientific inquiry. As a result, the work of science never ends; a scientific eschaton can never be reached, theoretically or practically.

The authority of science and of scientists takes on its own peculiar character. Science, as a nurturing agency of culture, makes certain demands. Michael Polanyi, writing about science, declares:

> The assimilation of great systems of articulate lore by novices of various grades is made possible by a previous act of affiliation, by which the novice accepts the apprenticeship to a community which cultivates this lore, appreciates its values, and strives to act by its standards. This affiliation begins with the fact that a child submits to education within a community, and it is confirmed throughout life to the extent to which the adult continues to place exceptional confidence in the intellectual leaders of the same community.[9]

In science subordination to its disciplines is necessary in order to achieve the cultivation required for understanding its intelligibilities, and also to make new discoveries or revolutionary breakthroughs from the given. A student engaged in an introduction to physics should be concerned primarily with the given lore of physics and not at that point with making a revolutionary discovery.

Authority, therefore, is invested in the given lore of science, and also in those persons who having been nurtured by it are now deserving of trust and respect for such cultivation and skill. The layperson assumes that he must trust such authority since he does not have the kind of cultivated experience or subjectivity that can unravel the "intelligibilities" of the various scientific disciplines. The novice scientist likewise must trust his teachers at least in the beginning of his education.

Authority is here seen as nurture focusing itself in scientific pursuits. The limits of science constitute the limits of such authority. Furthermore, the use of such language as trust implies a dimension of reality that is not scientific.

Authoritarianism in science can be seen from the adoption of status quo scientific perspectives as being the equivalent of complete knowledge, or from the identification of reality as understood by the methods of science with the whole of reality, known and unknown, or in the resistance to the many scientific revolutions which result in radical change and perspective in scientific inquiry itself. Such distorted postures eliminate the healthy tension between the universes of discourse and the prior universe of action and experience, and may result in the worship of science. Such scientism is the authoritarian expression in this contemplative focus on reality. Many important scientific breakthroughs were initially rejected by some members of the scientific community because of such an authoritarian posture.

Science cannot comprise the whole of what is the case. The world, as a whole, is not intelligible. This is why there are so many intelligibilities within science itself. Consequently, science is limited in scope. The responsible scientist is one who works within the universes of discourse called science, but as a person is distinguished from this nurturing agency.

It was the philosopher, Immanuel Kant, who made the statement that the world as a whole is not intelligible, i.e., available by means of the reductionism of the human technical reason. But, strangely enough, the world as a whole is imaginable. This occasions a consideration of the second sphere under contemplation: art.

One of the reasons for metaphysical confusion in the history of philosophy rests in the mistaken identity of an artistic image with an intelligible object of theoretical or scientific thought. Such an image as cosmos, for example, is derived from a predominantly aesthetic culture, Greece. The cosmos is the supremely ordered, harmonious whole. Yet such a concept of cosmos (in reality, an artistic image which can be imagined) cannot be thought. It cannot be an object of technical thought, because then it becomes one of many objects, and thus cannot be the whole. Metaphysical confusion arises between what is possible scientifically and what is possible artistically. If the latter aesthetic image is transformed into a scientific or theoretical object (as the Continental Rationalists indeed tried to do), the result is metaphysical confusion. As a result, all important metaphysical systems are speculative, imaginative experiments, and thus are more like works of art, than scientific universes of discourse limited by the reductionism of the theoretical or technical reason. This is not to say that artistic wholes are irrational; on the contrary, they are able to grasp what the "reduced reason" since the seventeenth century has neglected in its pursuits.

Art is one branch of cultural exertion. So inevitably even such an aesthetic image as cosmos must be distinguished from the universe of action and experience. It has its own peculiar shape derived from aesthetic formulation, and is thus dependent on culture. An artistic image such as cosmos cannot be the equivalent of the whole reality for this reason. It is a restricted whole derived from the aesthetic imagination. Speculative, cosmological systems, however, can serve as models for ultimate reality. Moreover, only artistic creativity can grasp wholes contemplatively in this restricted way; science cannot do this. In those times, however, when radical changes in scientific perspectives occur, visions of new models or images of reality become the basis for a different direction in scientific inquiry. Here artistic and imaginative creativity are the means used for the achievement of such radical breakthroughs and new directions. Consequently, art, speculation, and science meet in such creative action.

The work of art, however, whole that it is, is limited by the self-experience of its creator and the cultural matrix from which it arises. It is a reflection of that experience. Consequently, the whole world that is depicted by a work of art is just that, a pictured world, a semblance of wholeness. It is thus a contemplative world, and one artist even in a lifetime may create many such semblances.

The "worlds" of art can enrich our lives, can transform them, can grasp fragments and change them into a vision of wholeness. Art itself cultivates human experience in a different way from scientific cultivation. Whereas in science, the self must be subordinate to its methods and nurtured accordingly, resulting in a kind of detached subjectivity or reduced subjectivity which enables it to be "objective" in its evaluations and deliberations, so art cultivates subjectivity through coordinating the experience of the artist with the external referents in question. The way the artist experiences the world is very important, and often is expressed through the artistic medium. The highly creative artist may, however, create the illusion or semblance of some aspect of reality in such a way that it becomes a symbolic form without necessarily expressing in those moments of creativity his own experience, but with this as an exception, the depicted world of the artist is often filled up with the artist's personal experience and feeling, or with the experience and feeling available in the given cultural matrix. Science by necessity in its normal work must take the opposite route since the personal experience and feeling of the scientist is subordinated to science and its methods.

Such an emphasis on coordination determines the character of artistic authority. Art is designed to cultivate as much as possible wholeness in the person. The enrichment of personal life through the nurture of great art should be obvious, and yet its nurturing authority is dependent on the individual's sensitivity and feeling. Art can cultivate such feeling and yet paradoxically its authority rests on such feeling.

The healthy tension between culture as a nurturing agency and individual freedom and initiative is graphically portrayed in the life of great artists. A great artist is one who is a unique individual, who has made breakthroughs from his culture, and has thus enriched the cultural fabric with novelty of feeling and creation. And yet such a great artist also reflects his culture perhaps better than any other person. Nurture and experience are coordinated contemplatively in artistic work, and the definition of authority presented earlier is seen in such coordination.

Authoritarianism in artistic expression is found in aestheticism. All artistic wholeness is depicted or is a semblance of what is the case, and thus must be distinguished from the universe of action and experience. This constitutes the limits of art and its authority. When such a distinction is blurred, then, the artist or the devotee of art becomes victimized by such a human creation. It becomes difficult for such persons to discern the difference between depicted reality and the personal dimension, and the peculiar distortions of authority in this sphere begin to appear. Art is constituted by many depicted wholes; as a result, eschatological wholeness is not a possibility for art, except in terms of the creation of a semblance of such wholeness.

The area of contemplation comprises both science and art. They create in their own respective ways a multiplicity of universes of discourse, of intelligible and imaginable worlds, that contribute to an understanding of reality and that take their place as elements in the nurturing task of culture. As long as the many universes of discourse are not uncritically identified with the universe of action and experience, then both art and science express their authority through cultural nurture and cultivation.

The area of action which comprises politics and morality must now be considered. The political realm is analogous in this area to science in the contemplative area. As particular data are subordinated to the general concept in science in order to arrive at a probable factuality, so in politics the many selves or persons are unified, at least outwardly, through the many persons being citizens of a state to which they are subordinate. Here the inward life of each man and woman is less important than the organized group of selves achieved through an external structure known as a political community. The state is not a visible structure, but it is rather most accurately described as a universal self (esprit de corps) to which all individual persons are subject. The degree of flexibility in the state regarding subordination of the citizens will determine whether the state attempting to achieve a harmonious community will be a totalitarian and coercive power in which the individual counts as nothing except as an abstract unit expressing the social self of the state, or whether the state has built within it safeguards to such pretensions and depersonalizing tendencies.

Perfect community is never achievable politically, so a certain tension asserts itself between political structures on the one hand representing cultural nurture (or oppression), and the individual experience on the other representing the freedom of the person and his ability to breathe new forms, new direction, into status quo structures. An eschatologically whole community is not possible politically, since this would necessitate the total subordination of persons to the whole, and thus destroy freedom. This has often been the intention of utopian and totalitarian political schemes.

Political authority thus reflects the limits of political possibility. If all authority should nurture, then political structures are not exempted from this requirement. It is, however, true that political structures often take on the character of "ends in themselves" and because of the subordination necessary in political exertion, oppression and enslavement find their most obvious expression in the human political enterprise.

The possibilities for this are abundant, so perhaps one example will suffice. A political structure dedicated to freedom and based on noble principles devoted to the cultivating and nurturing of human beings shows its possibility for distortions in the struggle of Blacks in the United States. The structures were dedicated to nurture, but not nurture for all, only some. The safeguards against oppression, built into the structures, did not keep Blacks from being non-citizens and non-persons. The declaration of an articulate Black spokesman is particularly pertinent here: "They sing, 'My country 'tis of thee, sweet land of liberty.' But they do not mean blacks. This is the black man's paradox, the absurdity of living in a world with 'no rights which the white man is bound to respect.'"[10] The struggle for Black Power is a poignant example of the necessity for political structures to nurture and cultivate human beings, enabling them to become truly centered selves, and thus relatively free beings. When the status quo structures did not provide such nurture, it became necessary for the Black revolution in the United States to attempt to provide it. From the definition of authority expressed in this book, the struggle for Black Power is a "legitimate" revolutionary activity, since the given structures did not provide adequate nurture for black people, enabling them to become persons in their own right.

Political authority, therefore, is and must be a nurturing force. If it ceases to be this for any reason, resistance to such oppression and neglect is not resistance to authority but rather to authoritarian distortions. The healthy tension between authority and freedom must be maintained, and if one takes the American experiment seriously, such a tension is basic to the safeguards against oppression written into the Constitution of the United States.[11]

We now come to the moral sphere of human cultural exertion which constitutes the hidden action of the individual in the making of himself into a whole person. In this respect moral action is basic in all cultural areas. The element of trust that was found in the discussion of scientific authority illustrates the moral exertion implicit there. It is true of all other areas as well, since moral exertion is the hidden power of persons as they exert themselves culturally. Since the tension between culture and experience must be maintained, it is achieved through the impact of moral action. It is within moral action that the fundamental tension is conserved. Consequently, moral action is something vastly different from moralism.

Moralism is a failure to initiate responsible action. So often it is an adoption of current givens that is a betrayal of moral action. It may be said that any attempt on the part of the individual or a group to absolutize the relative structures of cultural exertion whether these are found in the contemplative areas of science and art, or in the active area of politics, or in what has come to be known as moral laws, is a betrayal of true moral action. Any system of moral law or morality that becomes itself a nurturing agency of culture and which at the same time demands absolute submission of the individual to itself is obviously attempting to deny the fundamental tension considered in this study: culture conditions and nurtures experience, but experience initiates and creates culture. Thus the moralist of this sort is really immoral. Such immorality results because of the denial of the possibility of moral action which is best exemplified by the healthy tension in question. Such immorality actually occasions moral passivity.

The human person finds himself within the complexity of the above analysis. He is, on the one hand, the product of the conditioning and nurturing agencies of culture. He may be only this. On the other hand, he may break through these conditioning agencies, and he may become an initiator and creator of cultural forms. The degree to which he is able to do this for himself and/or for the social groups of the culture in which he lives will determine the degree of his personhood and his freedom.

Moral authority, consequently, is rooted squarely in the healthy tension. The person who maintains the tension remains open to the future and its possibilities, and resists any attempts to destroy the tension by premature resolution of the moral struggle. Moralism, on the other hand, is an authoritarian distortion which attempts to deny the tension.

It may be concluded that the moral person is the relatively free person, seeking to become a centered self, and a whole person.[12] Is there any authority that the moral person can find in which to center his life and his personhood without falling into authoritarian distortions? P.T. Forsyth expresses it as follows: "The secret and unity of true personality is real faith in something, some authority, some creative and personal authority, that comes from without, lifts us out of our warring selves, and gives us a unity of reconciliation."[13] Hence our discussion of moral authority issues into the questions centering in religious authority; authority and faith.

NOTES: Chapter Four

1.   J.H. Randall, Jr., "Metaphysics and Language," The Review of Metaphysics, 20 (June 1967), p. 592. Used by permission of the editor.

2.   Ibid.

3.   Ibid., p. 593.

4.   Ludwig Wittgenstein, Philosophical Investigations, trans. by G.E.M. Anscombe (Oxford: Blackwell, 1958), pp. 11ff.

5.   Randall, op. cit., p. 593. Used by permission.

6.   This fundamental tension corresponds to the tensions between authority and freedom, universality and individuality, described earlier.

7.   Illich, op. cit., p. 27.

8.   For a more detailed evaluation of this analysis of culture based on the philosophy of Richard Kroner, see the author's Self and World (Philadelphia: University of Pennsylvania Press, 1962), pp. 55-86. Also Richard Kroner, Culture and Faith (Chicago: University of Chicago Press, 1951).

9.   Michael Polanyi, Personal Knowledge (New York: Harper Torchbooks, 1964), p. 207.

10.   James H. Cone, Black Theology and Black Power (New York: The Seabury Press, 1969), pp. 10-11. Used by permission of the publisher.

11.   See William J. Wolf, Freedom's Holy Light. American Identity and the Future of Theology (Wakefield, Massachusetts: Parameter Press, 1977).

12.   In this connection A. Sabatier declares: "Authority can maintain itself only by becoming more moral; by placing its supporting point always less apart from man, always more essentially within the man himself. The authority of material force, custom, tradition, the code,

more and more yields to the inward authority of conscience and the reason, and in the same measure becomes transformed for the subject into a true autonomy." op. cit., pp. xxvi-xxvii.

13.   P.T. Forsyth, op. cit., p. 29. Used by permission of the publisher.

CHAPTER FIVE

AUTHORITY AND FAITH

Moral action has certain ambiguous characteristics since it is maintained by the affirmation of the healthy tension described in past discussions. Can such a healthy tension be affirmed morally? This is an intriguing question, because moral action is precisely the maintenance of the tension, and yet without a reality transcending the tension in which the moral person may find himself centered, the tension tends to be denied in a number of ways.

It may be destroyed by lapsing into the protective cover of the cultural fabric through a conscious or unconscious acceptance of such a fabric as ultimate. Here the cultural fabric becomes the opiate of the people. Such a lapse involves a kind of commitment or act of faith which resolves prematurely this tension and it becomes the occasion for the authoritarian distortions which have been briefly mentioned earlier. Usually such commitment involves an embracing of the cultural fabric, or some portion of it, as the ultimate source of value for the person, regardless of how he may express this in mythological, cultural, or religious terms.

An additional possibility arises from the rejection of the peculiar cultural structures which have nurtured the person. Here no affirmation can be given that such a cultural fabric represents the ultimate source of value for the person; on the contrary, it is the enemy. From a posture of rebellion and resentment, the tension is destroyed. One's reason for being is found in intense defiance of the status quo structures in resistance to their authority or their power, and the basis for personhood is found in such defiance.[1]

The question, then, arises: Is there any reality which transcends cultural articulation, on the one hand, and the personal dimension, on the other? Presumably so; otherwise, reality would merely be the equivalent of human creation. It is not difficult to affirm such a transcending reality: rather, the difficulty emerges in describing the nature of such reality. To those who have been able in a variety of ways to transcend cultural intelligibilities and "view" this reality, a number of words have been used to describe it: abyss, void, being, becoming, the nature of things, fate, enemy, companion, God. Whatever the reality is called, it demands that human beings come to terms with it either by protecting themselves from it through the absolutizing of the cultural fabric, or some portion of it, or through defiance of it as an alien and rejecting power, or through acceptance of it as ultimately a benevolent and gracious reality. H. Richard Niebuhr articulates it as follows: "This reality, this nature of things, abides when all else passes. It is the source of all things and the end of all. It surrounds our life as the greatabyss into which all things plunge and as the great source whence they all come."[2]

A certain dilemma has developed in our argument. The definition of authority has been focused on the importance of nurture, and the development of centered persons who are relatively free. Presupposed in this definition is an implicit affirmation that reality is ultimately benevolent and accepting, that reality itself is the ultimate source of nurture for all, and for human beings in particular. Such an affirmation in Chapter One was the basis we used for accepting the Gospel criterion for determining the meaning of authority. If such is not the nature of reality, then, no acceptable reason can be given for maintaining "nurture and liberation" as the definition of authority expressed in nature and cultural forms, or in personal life. Presumably, if reality is not ultimately the source of nurture, or to put it in the language of Christian Faith, redemptive and liberating, then no safeguards against authoritarian distortions are possible, and the whole question of authority is either dissociated from reality which would make it illusory, or in conforming to reality would make it either neutral to human good, or alien to it. As a result, authority would have indeed disappeared, and the only thing remaining would be various forms of organized power. It is, therefore, obvious that the definition of authority in Chapter One has embodied within it many affirmations which have their origin from a posture of faith.

The sources of such faith have already been articulated in Chapter One. They are represented by a community of faith that itself has nurtured its members over many centuries. H. Richard Niebuhr describes this aptly:

> Now a strange thing has happened in our history and in our personal life; our faith has been attached to that great void, to that enemy of all our causes, to that opponent of all our gods. . . . We have been allowed to attach our confidence to it, and put our reliance in it which is the one reality beyond all the many, which is the last power. . . . And insofar as our faith. our reliance for meaning and worth, has been attached to this source and enemy of all our gods, we have been enabled to call this reality God.[3]

Niebuhr continues his explanation by describing one way in which this has happened in our history:

> There may be other ways but this is the usual way for us, that we confront in the event of Jesus Christ the presence of that last power which brings to apparent nothingness the life of the most loyal man. Here we confront the slayer, and here we become aware that this slayer is the life-giver. He does not put to shame those who trust in him. In the

presence of Jesus Christ we most often conceive, or are given that faith. We may try to understand how we might have received the faith without Jesus Christ, but the fact remains that when this faith was given Jesus Christ was there.[4]

A great deal more may be said, and has been said, about this affirmation which is rooted in the Christian Gospel. "In the beginning was the Word," said St. John,[5] and that Word was made flesh in Jesus Christ. The nature of the transcending reality is benevolent and accepting, that which is the source of all being is also the source of all meaning and value, and this reality is definitively focused and revealed in the events related to Jesus Christ.

From the posture of such faith and through the adoption of the Gospel criterion, it has been concluded that the quest of human beings as this is evidenced in the tension between culture and experience is an endless one. Culture can never arrive at the point where a "whole reality" can be completely claimed without pretension. Moreover, the moral action of the individual in the attempt to achieve wholeness of personality is also an unending task, and, as it was concluded earlier, often accompanied by sinful distortions. Such wholeness, whether it is cultural or individual, has a certain eschatological character.

It is the claim of the Christian Gospel that in the revelation of Jesus Christ, wholeness arises in the midst of the fragmented attempts of cultural and personal exertion. In Jesus Christ the wholeness of the hidden God is manifest. Thus the old creation becomes new when seen from such a revelatory focus. Being and value are identified. The creation becomes whole both in retrospect and in prospect.

Thus the dilemma centering around the definition of authority comes full circle. It cannot be denied that circular reasoning is present. The question does arise, however, as to what the alternatives may be. If reality, and the nature of reality, is related to the whole question of authority in all of its expressions, then a posture of faith is implicit in whatever views are developed concerning authority. If reality is not ultimately redemptive, then the tasks of culture and its so-called authorities may be to protect human beings from reality. It is difficult to understand how any person could hold to such a position, but a great deal of such protection is now being offered by a variety of cultural expressons: scientism, aestheticism, statism, moralism, and ecclesiasticism. Here obviously authority has disappeared and organized protective and/or oppressive power has taken over.

At the same time, a posture of defiance may express itself against oppressive cultural structures; it may also take on the dimension of a defiance against alien reality. But such a posture is itself rooted in a certain kind of faith and perhaps in a certain kind of

revelatory focus; reality revealed as alien and rejecting.[6] Traditionally, this experience of ultimate rejection has resulted in the personification of such alien reality as Satan, and in some instances the God who
was supposedly the source of authority becomes identified with Satan,
the symbol of coercion and rejection.

So perhaps the circle is unavoidable, and the conclusion not wholly
to be resisted that even in large segments of secular culture in the
West, the Judaeo-Christian revelation of the nature of reality is
implicitly affirmed, albeit without the traditional language. If this is
true, then, P.T. Forsyth is correct when he declares: "We have no
absolute authority over us except in our faith; and without it, all
relative authority becomes more and more relative and less and less
authoritative. There is no final answer to the question of any authority
but the answer contained in our personal faith."[7]

Granted, then, that access to ultimate reality comes through
faith; and that faith for Christians was given in Jesus Christ; and he
becomes the center or focus for the ultimate; and from this focus, the
nature of the ultimate (God) is revealed as benevolent and accepting;[8]
the question of the meaning of authority for Christians, as a result,
must have its issue from such a focus and from such an affirmation.
The source of such a faith, therefore, involves the following:

> The encounter with transcendence that constitutes the
> basis of religious conviction never occurs without the medi-
> ation of some created agency -- the humanity of Christ, the
> Church, the Scriptures, the Sacraments, or whatever. Thus
> even when one appropriates the Christian faith with the
> fullness of personal conviction, one remains dependent on
> external signs to present and commend the content of faith.
> An element of authority remains.[9]

Or another way of expressing this insight is: "The person of Jesus
Christ is ever itself the cornerstone of all testimony regarding Him, but
the evidence which is valid from age to age goes back to it, not through
the void, but through the peace and joy and holiness it has wrought in
the souls of men in all ages, from which we may not exclude our
own."[10]

If the preceding discussion is correct, then, access to ultimate
reality comes through the peculiar function of created agencies,
namely, for Christians, the Church, and such an agency becomes a
nurturing force for the cultivation of human personhood. The Church,
as a nurturing agent, insofar as it reflects the culture of its time and
place, is a part of human culture and subject to all the limitations and
criticism that any other branch of human culture is subject. As a
nurturing agent, it is not absolute. It is to cultivate, not to smother; it
is to serve, not to be served; it is to fight oppression, not to be the

agent of oppression; it is to liberate, and not to enslave. It is as Avery Dulles declares:

> Christianity recognizes only one absolute authority -- that of God Himself. This means that all secondary authorities are subject to criticism and correction. Every created channel that manifests God and brings men to him is capable also of misleading men and turning them away from God. If the secondary authorities were absolutized, Christianity would fall into idolatry.[11]

Three dimensions of authority centering around the revelatory focus in Jesus Christ arise as the community which responded to that gracious focus takes shape. Gordon D. Kaufman approaches these three dimensions by applying the authority of the historian, since the reality given in Jesus Christ was indeed given in history. Kaufman notes that (a) the historian cannot avoid giving great weight to his secondary sources which provide him with an indispensable orientation. These sources are of course constituted by a dynamic tradition. Also, (b) the historian must always consider the primary sources, even though these sources do not interpret themselves. These sources are Holy Scriptures. And, finally, (c) the authority of the historian himself must be brought into account. This is the source of experience.[12]

Here Kaufman sets out in historical terms the important tension described earlier. Scripture and Tradition are historical givens in relation to the revelatory event. They constitute the pole of nurture when considering the posture of faith. At the same time, the importance of the experiential cannot be diminished. The personal experience is shaped by Tradition and Scripture, but since they point to a reality transcending themselves, the personal experience may gain new insights into the reality which hitherto have been locked in the agencies of Scripture and Tradition.[13] If this is not the case, then, Scripture and Tradition become fixed and rigid, the dynamic element is lost, and forms of religious oppression begin. Thus the authority of Scripture and Tradition is derived from the revelatory focus, and it is basic to the nuture of faith, but personal experience also plays a role. The role of personal experience is especially embraced by John Oman when he states:

> We must ask how the authority of the Church, from which we have received so much and by which we have been largely fashioned, is brought into unity with the authority within, which is the evidence of a spiritual hope, and how, in their perfect harmony, we can realize our service and our freedom."[14]

The unity which Oman affirms is eschatological. It is the basis for human hope that in the posture of faith all will be consummated in

the end in the benevolent acceptance and love of God. This eschata-
logical hope is in tension with the actual state of human beings as
described in this book. The reality of such a final unity can be hoped
for, but life must be lived in the midst of the healthy tension. The final
resolution of the predicament comes through the initiative of God, and
not through human projections, even if such projections are based on
the language of faith.

The authority of the Church as a nurturing agent, therefore, takes
on a peculiar status. It is indeed anchored in the revelatory focus of
Jesus Christ. Consequently, it is expressed by the witness of Holy
Scripture and the continuing interpretation of a living and dynamic
tradition. It has served to nourish personal faith, and to cultivate
personhood. But the nature of its authority is, or should be, different
from other agencies. Dietrich Bonhoeffer explains:

> Is it not characteristic of the Church's authority (distin-
> guishing it from all other authority) that the Church does
> not have the authority first and then acts upon it, but that
> she gains it through proclaiming God's commands, and to the
> extent that they are accepted as being his commands, and
> that with every word spoken she puts her authority at risk?
> The authority of the state does not rest in concrete deci-
> sions, but the authority of the Church does, entirely. But
> she must not fail to make decisions through fear of this risk
> and of possible chaos. . . . And this quite apart from the
> fact that, in a case whereby some catastrophically mistaken
> decision the Church's authority may really be lost, a quite
> different authority becomes visible, which is that of God's
> mercy.[15]

Another way of stating this is: "The Gospel of Christ's Cross is
therefore the final center of all authority, because there alone the
Holiness of God -- the absolute sublimity, transcendence, and victory of
the God of conscience -- establishes itself forever in the destruction of
both guilt and sin. We transcend our immanence only morally -- by
redemption.[16]

The sources of the Church's authority, consequently, are found in
its acts of proclaiming the Gospel, and the Gospel is rooted in a Cross
which stands as the sublime symbol of that authority. The Church,
therefore, stands before the Cross, and paradoxically, the more the
Church offers herself as the servant, the more authority she is given
from the ultimate source, but it is an authority given by way of the
Cross.

The peculiar distortions of the authority of the Church express
themselves in the attempt to achieve authority out of herself as an
ecclesiastical-political structure, serving not the Lord, but rather

serving herself as one of the competing institutions of culture. It is in this context that Ivan Illich's statement is helpful: "To live up to this task the Church must recognize that she is growing powerless to orient and produce development. The less efficient she is as a power the more effective she can be as a celebrant of the mystery."17

In conclusion, from within the celebration of the mystery of the nurturing and redeeming presence of God can come the recognition that genuine authority is the opposite of coercive power. Consequently, power without authority is coercion, destructive and demonic; authority without coercion is precisely the creative and nurturing matrix which has as its issue, personhood and freedom. To express this in traditional theological imagery, authority without coercive power is the grace of God; power without authority is the coercive action of Satan.

NOTES: Chapter Five

1. These two examples traditionally can be seen as descriptions of human sinfulness expressed by pride and sensuality. We have already seen this in our discussion of Kierkegaard's The Sickness Unto Death, and in the twentieth century Reinhold Niebuhr's remarkable insights here are well known.

2. H. Richard Niebuhr, Radical Monotheism and Western Culture (New York: Harper and Brothers, 1960), p. 122. Used by permission of the publisher.

3. Ibid., pp. 122-123. Used by permission of the publisher.

4. Ibid., pp. 124-125. Used by permission of the publisher.

5. Gospel according to John 1.1.

6. The positive aspect of the Black Power movement has already been affirmed. In the same development, however, a posture of defiance to oppression tends to become almost an ultimate if not the ultimate for the movement. As J.H. Cone states it: "Black Theology sees a prior authority that unites all black people and transcends these theological differences. . . . To put it simply, Black Theology knows no authority more binding than the experience of oppression itself. This alone must be the ultimate authority in religious matters." Op. cit., p. 120. Used by permission of the publisher. If this is rhetoric, then it is excusable, but as theology, it is highly questionable. The ultimate authority transcends the experience of oppression and rests in redemption from oppression, and such redemption or liberation as we have seen is itself rooted in the nature of reality itself.

7. Forsyth, op. cit., p. 11. Used by permission.

8.   For an excellent discussion of the many difficulties involved in such an affirmation, see Gordon D. Kaufman, God the Problem (Cambridge: Harvard University Press, 1972).

9.   Avery Dulles, The Survival of Dogma (New York: Doubleday and Company, 1971), pp. 42-43.

10.   John Oman, Vision and Authority (London: Hodder and Stoughton, 1902), p. 199.

11.   Dulles, op. cit., p. 84.

12.   Gordon D. Kaufman, Systematic Theology. A Historicist Perspective (New York: Charles Scribner's Sons, 1968), pp. 67-69. Another way of presenting this material can be found in Rupert Davies' scheme. The Holy Scriptures, he sees, as the Apostolic Tradition. The Catholic Tradition is based on and develops out of the apostolic; it is embodied in the liturgies of the great Churches, in the ecumenical Creeds, and the Confessions and Articles of the great Communions, and further expounded by the Schoolmen and the great Reformers. He next speaks of the Confessional Traditions, Roman, Orthodox, and Protestant, and finally, of the Denominational Traditions, some local and some national in scope. Religious Authority in an Age of Doubt (London: Epworth Press, 1968), pp. 26-28.

13.   Here the work of the Holy Spirit as transcending both Scripture and Tradition is often affirmed.

14.   Oman, op. cit., p. 91.

15.   In a letter from Dietrich Bonhoeffer to Helmuth Roessler. Quoted by Mary Bosanquet in The Life and Death of Dietrich Bonhoeffer (New York: Harper and Row, 1968), pp. 94-95. Used by permission.

16.   Forsyth, op. cit., pp. 364-365. Used by permission.

17.   Illich, op., cit., p. 97.

CHAPTER SIX

AUTHORITY AND THEOLOGICAL RECONSTRUCTION

Theological reflection is a legitimate activity of persons within a community which affirms its roots in a revelatory constellation of events, and which therefore desires to make explicit what such a communal and personal response to revelatory events involves. We have concluded that authority has its ultimate origins from such a posture of faith and the sources of it are to be found in the "objects" of such faith. For Christians the ultimate source of authority is in the revealed Divine Reality, the God disclosed in the revelatory focus of Jesus Christ. When Christians affirm that disclosure, affirm that the Word which was from the beginning became flesh in a definitive way in Jesus of Nazareth, we can then also ascertain that the Word of God, the self-disclosure of the Divine Reality, is a creative and redemptive activity which expresses itself both in nature and in history, and as mediated, it is a nurturing and liberating presence at work subtly in nature, in history, and in the various cultural fabrications of reality achieved through human action.

Authority, therefore, which is derived ultimately from the Divine Reality, the Word of God, must itself be that expression in a variety of ways. The degree to which a nurturing and liberating presence is mediated determines the degree to which authority prevails. Road-blocks to such mediation due to faulty views of reality, pretentious claims for the cultural fabric, and sinful distortions both social and personal, result in the disappearance of authority, of the nurturing and liberating presence, and the sheer power of a smothering oppression takes over; coercion prevails over nurture and liberation.

The tasks of theological reflection in such a context are never-ending. A constant process of theological reconstruction is necessary in order to avoid an alien blockage of the authority derived from the Divine Reality -- a blockage often coming from the communities supposedly committed to such an authority. When this happens the nurturing and liberating presence becomes a judgment on the sinful pretensions responsible for the blockage.

At the present time theological reconstruction should take place within the aforementioned context of an affirmation of authority as the nurturing and liberating presence of the Divine Reality, and also within the contemporary context of a growing awareness of limits, limits, to nature, limits to human life, and limits to the possible growth that can occur through our cultural exertion without resulting in the eventual destruction both of nature and of human beings. As Charles Birch has observed: "The world is a Titanic on a collision course. The iceberg ahead has its visible parts above water. . . . We do not know how many more people, if any more, the earth can provide for. We know that there is a limit which is being approached, if not already exceeded."[1]

This would seem to indicate the need to put the brakes on the technological exploitation of natural resources; this would seem to demand that we see ourselves as emergents from the creative natural process, and not as some strange intruders from without. It indicates the need to reaffirm an interdependent relationship which characterizes all of reality; an interdependence which contributes to the wholeness of being rather than to its premature destruction.

Theological reconstruction should, then, go on within a context of certain basic affirmations and certain needed negations. First, there should be an affirmation of mutual interdependence on the human level; a development of Buber's intersubjective dynamic; a healing of the alienation within human selfhood particularly as this was occasioned by faulty views of reality derived from seventeenth century perspectives; and a removal of many obstacles which prohibit an interdependence of person and person.

All of this speaks to our need to cultivate an intersubjective dynamic which will contribute to a communion of souls. In this context, therefore, we must deny images of selfhood such as those produced by the Cartesian reduction of personhood to the status of thinking thing, or the tormented isolation and alienation asserted in some existentialist images of human selfhood. Furthermore, a negation of behaviorial theories which are obviously mechanistic is in order, as well as a rejection of the many collective group involvements which transform human selfhood into a mere reflection of the social self of the dominant group. Consequently, an affirmation of self-initiative within a context of social responsibility is the first step towards a communion of souls.

Secondly, an affirmation of interdependence and communion in relation to nature is very much in order. We must view human beings as unique emergents from the creative natural process. We must cultivate a renewal of feeling for the various areas of nature; a respect for nature; a guarded use of natural resources; and the adoption of an attitude of conservation in which not only human needs are considered, but also the needs of other creatures as well. Here the discovery of a sacramental relation to nature will result in the affirmation of Smuts' declaration that "the field of nature is the source of the grand ecology of the universe. It is the vital, friendly, educative and creative environment for all wholes, and all souls."

In contrast to this, we must stand in judgment upon the exploiter, the waster, the destroyer of nature. Human beings must obviously use the resources of nature in order to survive, but the use of such resources can be controlled by a respect and regard for all natural reality; a negation of the wanton and irresponsible ravishing of such resources. In this way, the cultivation of human selfhood, self-initiative and social responsiblity, will also contribute to the cultivation of a respect and regard for the environment in which we live; and a concern for the nurture and care of all the participants in the natural world; social responsibility extended to the fulness of nature and human being.

Such affirmations, and also such negations, are very much in harmony with the lessons provided by the Second Report to the Club of Rome. Here we are admonished to develop a world consciousness in which each individual is a member of an international community, and self-initiative and social responsibility are extrapolated on a world scale. We are also enjoined to develop an ethic in the use of resources based on minimal use and the longevity of products rather than the wanton and irresponsible current usage. We must view nature in a different light from the current emphasis on domination and exploitation. Finally, all creatures, present and future, should be cared for and considered when we use the natural gifts presented to us for our nourishment and continuing existence.[2]

In these days without the recognition and approval of such a nurturing context for theological reconstruction, it is difficult to understand how one could engage in theologizing or any other conceptual endeavor. When people are living on the margin of existence; when life which is a bid for freedom is forced back into the vast abyss of natural necessity; when the future is being destroyed by the rape of nature in the present; as human beings, as Christians, we are faced with certain fundamental or elemental tasks. We do not have the resources to luxuriate in verbal maneuvers and effete ratiocination. Rather, we should affirm theologically what will in a modest but perhaps effective way help us to realize what our previously discussed affirmations and negations present.

Consequently, if we are to affirm a communion of souls, and this seems to be one of the principal tenets of the Christian Gospel, we must be willing to give up our tendency towards theological exclusiveness in favor of a more universal reference. In this connection, as Christians, we shall continue to believe in Jesus of Nazareth as the unique focal point for the revelation of God, for here ultimacy is wedded to vivid immediacy. But we should also, in the spirit of that same Gospel and the authority derived from it, affirm the possibility of other such foci. By the very commitment we have to Jesus of Nazareth we are obligated to open our hearts, souls, and minds to persons in other traditions and cultures. Despotic Christian behavior; the impossible marriage of the Gospel with the dominant images of God as Imperial Caesar and ruthless moralist, which results in the use of coercive power to destroy not only dissent but also fundamental differences in human belief; all of this which is so much a part of our Christian past should be offered up to the Divine Reality who will judge it and return it to us with the tenderness and wisdom which saves even the most arrogant and destructive powers.

One example of this sort of Christian arrogance can be seen in the long history of implicit, and often explicit, anti-Semitism in Christian practice. In order to develop a communion of souls, we should again as Christians affirm our Jewish past, embrace our Jewish brothers and sisters, and at the same time, affirm the novelty that has arisen in the revelation of God in Jesus of Nazareth, himself a Jew. One of our Jewish brothers, Martin Buber, has helped us in this by his attraction to Jesus as the model of the human relationship to God.

Furthermore, another aspect of the affirmation of a communion of souls is seen in the present groping of women to receive the kind of recognition which mutual interdependence entails. Theologically, we should be aware of the way in which past imagery and doctrines have served as oppressive instruments in keeping women from realizing the fulness of possibility inherent in human personhood within a Christian context. The image of an omnipotent, impassible, immutable, Caesar-god is unacceptable to the Gospel of Christ, and yet such an image keeps lurking in the background of our theology and of our worship. It not only serves as an obstacle to understanding God as revealed in Jesus of Nazareth, but also it serves as a potentially, and at times actually, oppressive intrument in relation to the reality of womanhood.

As such an image of God tends to reinforce despotic, coercive behavior among individuals and states, a kind of Satan with us, it also indirectly serves as an obstacle to the development of interpersonal, mutually interdependent relationships between men and women. A communion of souls is best expressed in such relationships. It is not that such relationships have not happened and will not happen, but the obstacles are powerful and often prohibitive.

We have not seriously entertained the possibility of the kind of effect a reconstructed view of God, such as Whitehead's, would have on the cultivation of intersubjectivity, on self-initiative and social respon-sibility, on the human relationship to the creative natural process, and on the equation of authority with nurture and redemption rather than with coercion and oppression. As human beings, we feel more secure with a despotic God since in terms of our particular commitment to such a deity, we assume that such an all powerful being will accept us, and exclude our enemies, thus protecting us from all the rest who are not truly and faithfully believers in such a source of power and strength.

In this connection the imagery of a despotic Caesar-god also serves as an obstacle to the cultivation of a sacramental relationship with nature. Human beings, made in the image of such a powerful figure, themselves assume dominance over nature, and over one an-other, assuming that they are not themselves emergents from the creative natural process, but rather specially created images of the all powerful Caesar-god. The world, then, becomes merely the stage for the human drama, and as a stage, is fundamentally unimportant in comparison to the actors and actresses in the drama. The focus is almost exclusively on the human being, and this kind of egocentric predicament is well-known, philosophically and theologically.

In conclusion, what theological affirmations need to be made in order to begin a process which will correct some of the aberrations of the past. Several come to mind and they can serve as a modest starting-point for the difficult tasks we now face:

1. We must transform the imagery and models we use of God into an imagery derived more centrally from the Judaeo-Christian tradition, and also develop an imagery within the context of our groping together for new possibilities of communion. Our models of God must be understood precisely as models. We should not confuse the model with the reality mediated to us by it. The model Jesus used of God as a loving father, strong in his providential direction, but tempered by his care and concern, and his love for all, is still an important way for the ultimate reality to be mediated to us. Jesus' affectionate expression, Abba Father, which can come out as "Daddy" in contemporary parlance, conveys the kind of interdependent relationship we have been discussing. It also merges masculine and feminine aspects of ultimacy, the loving father is a loving person, and for this reason should not be seen as coercive or oppressive. A dismissal of such an image, because it is masculine, is misguided. It confuses the model with the reality.

At the same time, the development of models of deity using feminine imagery rather than male imagery is certainly to be encouraged. Here again the model is not the reality, but mediates the reality to us. It will be difficult for some of us to think of God expressed through the feminine imagery because of our involvement over the years with the distortion of the loving father image becoming rather a despotic father image. Such an image has contributed to making women subservient to him and also to all men. But the possibility of feminine models does not conflict with what we are given in the revelation of God in Jesus of Nazareth. We must be willing to open up ourselves to the possibility of such a vision of God. Since the cycles of nature are now seen as a creative process, marked by the emergence of novelty, rather than as the cyclical prison of the ancients, God expressed through feminine imagery may be recognized as being closer to the God of Biblical Tradition, than to the fertility goddesses of ancient times who were personifications of natural necessity from which the Gospel has freed us. In both instances, however, the loving God's reality is mediated through such models, participates in them, but is not exhausted by them.

Finally, abstractions denoting universality should be avoided. When ultimacy is wedded to vivid immediacy, the result is something quite particular, quite individual, quite unique, which because of the intensity of what it represents and mediates, conveys the reality of ultimacy and universality in and through itself. This is the only possible concrete universal.

2. Even though we must insist on models of deity which are not abstractly universal, at the same time, we should not permit such models to represent a being coming to us from without, as a strange intruder riding the clouds of heaven in a gigantic rescue task. When this happens, the idea of coercive power is reinforced, as in times of crisis, the omnipotent lord comes in with his legion of angels and cleans up the difficulties caused by human sinners. Instead, we should insist upon an important point in our tradition, the ultimate unity of creation and redemption; the goodness of the creation; in secular terms, the identification of fact and value. In this kind of affirmation we can visualize the healing, salvific action of God as being expressed in and through the creative natural process. Smuts' creative thrust and Whitehead's initial aim derived from the primordial nature of deity affirm that the creative process is fundamentally a redemptive and healing process, and that the power of such a healing is seen in the action of God in and through the process itself. If we can make such an affirmation as this, we shall be on the way to affirming a sacramental relationship to nature as well as a communion of souls, and on the human level of emergence which comes out as the drama of history, a view of God's action both in nature and in human history.

3. Finally, our last affirmation should attempt to unite nature, human beings, and our models of God in terms of a healthy wholeness. This affirmation can come from one segment of the tradition already developed and it may be expressed succinctly as: finitum capax infiniti (the finite is capable of the infinite). Such an affirmation makes possible what we have already discussed in relation to models of deity and the action of God in and through the creative process. It also affirms the possiblity of holy communion which is the most intimate kind of intersubjectivity, the possibility of real presence, in the dynamic of human persons to nature as Thou (not as It), and of human beings to God in and through the models developed in response to revelatory foci. Its opposite, finitum non capax infiniti (the finite is not capable of the infinite), which is also a part of our inherited tradition, tends to encourage views of human intrusion on the natural scene, and dominance over nature since the human being is constituted by the tension between finitude/infinitude and thus the human being is at least partially dissociated from the natural scene. Such a perspective also encourages the point of view of rescue efforts from without the creative natural process; God the stormy intruder, the coercive power which solves all crises and all problems fundamentally by being unrelated to them, except on certain momentous revelatory occasions.

It fosters a kind of modified Deism, the remote and isolated God acting only in certain crises. Theologically, it is the counterpart of the Cartesian dichotomy.

Such affirmations as the above should result in the kind of theological reconstruction which will be responsive to the issues and problems of our present context, and which may result in our rediscovery of the presence of authority in our midst; an authority issuing in nurture and liberation, and standing as judge on all coercion and oppression.

NOTES: Chapter Six

1.   Charles Birch, "Creation, Technology and Human Survival," An unpublished paper (address) delivered before the World Council of Churches in Nairobi, Kenya, p. 2.

2.   Mihajho Mesarovic and Eduard Pestel, Mankind at the Turning Point (New York: E.P. Dutton and Company, Inc., 1974), p. 147.

3.   The Old Testament witnesses speak out so strongly on this question that one wonders at the frequent attribution of the image of God as despot to the prophets. The tenderness of Hosea, in which God aches for, yearns for, His children stands as a profound testimony to the vision of deity which we have been attempting to develop. See Hosea 11:3-4; 8-9. Even the angry Jeremiah speaks of the meaning of God's loving paternity. See Jeremiah 31:9. In addition the Law of God does not stand alone. it is coupled with a reminder of the mercy of the Lord. See Amos 5:15.

SELECT BIBLIOGRAPHY

Among the vast number of resources available relating to the various aspects concerning the meaning of authority, the following have been most helpful in the preparation for this study.

General

Adorno, T.W. et. al.   *The Authoritarian Personality.* New York: Harper and Row, 1950.

Adelmann, F.J.   *Authority.* The Hague: M. Nijhoff, 1974.

Arendt, Hannah   *Origins of Totalitarianism.* New York: Harcourt Press, 1958.

—————————   *Between Past and Future.* New York: Viking Press, 1961.

—————————   "What Was Authority," *Authority*, edited by Carl J. Friedrich. Cambridge: Harvard University Press, 1958. Designated as *Nomos* I in following sources.

Berger, Peter & Luckman, T.L.   *The Social Construction of Reality.* Garden City: Doubleday, 1966.

Bryson, Lyman (ed.)   *Freedom and Authority in our Time.* Twelfth Symposium on the Conference on Science, Philosophy and Religion. New York: Harpers, 1953. Also edited by L. Finkelstein and R.M. MacIver.

Catlin, George E.G.   "Authority and its Critics," *Nomos* I.

Cone, James H.   *Black Theology and Black Power.* New York: Seabury Press, 1969.

Davies, Rupert E.   *Religious Authority in an Age of Doubt.* London: Epworth Press, 1968.

Dulles, Avery   *The Survival of Dogma.* New York: Doubleday and Company, 1971.

Easton, David   "The Perception of Authority and Political Change," *Nomos* I.

73

Forsyth, P.T.	The Principle of Authority. London: Independent Press, 1952.
Freire, Paulo	Pedagogy of the Opressed. New York: Herder and Herder, 1972.
Friedrich, Carl J.	"Authority, Reason and Discretion," Nomos I.
Gutierrez, Gustavo	A Theology of Liberation. History, Politics and Salvation. Maryknoll, N.Y.: Orbis Books, 1973.
Hall, Jerome	"Authority and the Law," Nomos I.
Hendel, Charles W.	"An Exploration of the Nature of Authority," Nomos I.
Hoebel, E.A.	"Authority in Primitive Societies," Nomos I.
Jacobsen, Norman	"Knowledge, Tradition and Authority: A Note on the American Experience," Nomos I.
Meissner, W.W.	The Assault on Authority. Maryknoll, N.Y.: Orbis Books, 1971.
Milgram, Stanley	Obedience to Authority. New York: Harper and Row, 1974.
Nash, Paul	Authority and Freedom in Education. New York: Wiley, 1966.
Oman, John	Vision and Authority. London: Hodder and Stoughton, 1902.
Parker, Thomas D.	"Authority Today: A Reconsideration," Union Seminary Quarterly Review, Vol. XXVI, No. 3, Spring, 1971.
Polanyi, Michael	Personal Knowledge. New York: Harper Torchbooks, 1964.
Quesnell, Quentin	The Authority for Authority. Milwaukee: Marquette University, 1973.
Rawlinson, A.E.J.	Authority and Freedom. London: Longmans, Green and Co., 1924.

Rice, C.E.
Authority and Rebellion. New York: Doubleday and Co., 1971.

Roszak, Theodore
The Making of a Counter Culture. Garden City: Doubleday, 1969.

Russell, Bertrand
Authority and the Individual. New York: Simon, 1949.

Sabatier, Auguste
Religions of Authority and Religions of the Spirit. New York: McClure, Phillips and Co., 1904.

Simon, Yves R.
A General Theory of Authority. Notre Dame: University of Notre Dame Press, 1962.

_____
Nature and Function of Authority. Milwaukee: Marquette University, 1940.

Thouless, R.H.
Authority and Freedom. Greenwich: Seabury Press, 1954.

Verghese, T.P.
The Freedom of Man. Philadelphia: Westminster Press, 1972.

Weber, Max
On Charisma and Institution Building. Chicago: University of Chicago Press, 1968.

Wolff, R.P.
In Defense of Anarchism. New York: Harper and Row, 1970.

Yarnold, G.D.
By What Authority? London: A.R. Mowbray Company, 1964.

Authority: Bible.

Berkouwer, G.C.
Studies in Dogmatics: Holy Scripture. Grand Rapids: Eerdmans, 1975.

Bright, John
Authority of the Old Testament. London: SCM Press, 1967.

Dodd, C.H.
Authority of the Bible. London, Nisbet, 1952.

Goudge, H.L.
The Church and the Bible. London: Longman, Green, and Co., 1930.

Hebert, A.G.   Authority of the Old Testament. London:
                           Faber and Faber, 1947.

Ramsey, A.M.   Authority of the Bible. London: Nelson,
                           1962.

Malden, R.H.   Authority of the New Testament. London:
                           Oxford University Press, 1937.

Authority: Church and Tradition.

Campenhausen, Hans   Ecclesiastical Authority and Spiritual
                           Power in the Church of the First Three
                           Centuries. Stanford: Stanford University
                           Press, 1969.

Dulles, Avery   Models of the Church. Garden City:
                           Doubleday and Company, 1974.

Harrison, Paul M.   Authority and Power in the Free Church
                           Tradition. Princeton: Princeton Universtiy
                           Press, 1959.

Jenkins, Daniel   Tradition, Freedom and the Spirit.
                           Philadelphia: Westminster Press, 1951.

Kung, Hans   The Church. New York: Sheed and Ward,
                           1968.

_____   Infallible? New York: Doubleday, 1972.

Lacey, T.A.   Authority in the Church. London: A.R.
                           Mowbray and Co., 1928.

Morrison, K.F.   Tradition and Authority in the Western
                           Church. Princeton: Princeton University
                           Press, 1969.

Rich, E.C.   Spiritual Authority in the Church of
                           England. London: Longmans and Green
                           Co., 1953.

Sanks, T.H.   Authority in the Church. Missoula:
                           Scholars Press, 1974.

Williams, R.R.   Authority in the Church. London: SPCK,
                           1965.

Power.

Guardini, R.   Power   and   Responsibility.   Chicago:
                                Regnery, 1961.

Hocking, W.E.   Man and the State.   New Haven: Yale
                                University Press, 1926.

de Jouvenel, Bertrand   Sovereignty.   Chicago: University   of
                                Chicago Press, 1957.

Lasswell H. and   The ethic of power. New York: Harper
Cleveland, H.   and Row, 1962.

May, Rollo   Power and Innocence.   New York: Norton,
                                1972.

Moore, Barrington Jr.   Political   Power   and   Social   Theory.
                                Cambridge: Harvard   University   Press,
                                1958.

Niebuhr, Reinhold   Moral Man and Immoral Society.   New
                                York: Scribner's, 1932.

Powell, Cyrus H.   The Biblical Concept of Power.   London:
                                Epworth Press, 1963.

Russell, Bertrand   Power: A New Social Analysis. New York:
                                Norton, 1938.

Sampson, Ronald W.   The Psychology of Power.   New York:
                                Pantheon Books, 1966.

Schermerhorn, R.A.   Society and Power.   New York: Random
                                House, 1965.

Tillich, Paul   Love, Power and Justice.   New York:
                                Oxford University Press, 1954.

ABOUT THE

John E. Skinner has been Holy
Episcopal Divinity School, Cambridg
to that he has taught at Temple
School, and the University of Penn
visiting professor at Crozer
Pennsylvania and at Lancaster
Pennsylvania. He was vice pr
Society from 1970-1971 and se
from 1971-1977. He has pub'
(1962) and The Logocentric
The New Dimension of the
has contributed a chapter, "An in
Sprituality, edited by W.J. Wolf, and publis